Portraits from North American Indian Life

Portraits from North American Indian Life

Edward S. Curtis

Introductions by

A. D. COLEMAN
and
T. C. McLUHAN

A&W Visual Library

Library of Congress Catalog Card Number: 74-33775
ISBN: 0-89104-003-X
Reprinted by arrangement with Outerbridge & Lazard, Inc.
Printed in the United States of America.

Grateful acknowledgment is hereby made for the assistance of the following people in gathering the material in this book:

Imogene Cunningham; Mrs. Florence Graybill; the staff of the Southwest Museum Research Library, Los Angeles; the librarians at the Seattle Public Library, Seattle; the staff at the Rare Book Division of the New York Public Library; M. E. Magnuson; Robert Monroe, Chief, Special Collections Division, Suzzallo Library, University of Washington, Seattle; Bill Holm, Burke Museum, University of Washington, Seattle.

CURTIS: HIS WORK

by A.D. Coleman

Edward S. Curtis created a work so monumental that it buried itself for more than fifty years.

Curtis certainly didn't intend it that way; his purpose in making *The North American Indian* was to document all aspects of a marvelous culture which was being inexorably destroyed, in such a way as to retain the spirit of that culture and keep it alive. Yet, in retrospect, it seems inevitable that this towering accomplishment should have fallen into obscurity for half a century, just as it seems fitting that the rediscovery of this work should be taking place at this particular juncture in history.

The neglect which *The North American Indian* has suffered has been, in a peculiar way, its own fault. Certainly it is not attributable to either willful blindness or accidental oversight on the part of the public. The project received an enormous amount of attention in the press, garnering reviews which were, quite rightly, lavish in their praise. And, preceding publication of the first volumes, Curtis arranged several very well-attended exhibits of his images—one of which, at the Waldorf–Astoria, brought in more than $1,300 in print sales, a high figure even today.

No, the problem with Curtis' work was not its visionary prematurity but its built-in disappearance potential. The cost of the entire undertaking was roughly one million dollars. When completed, the publication consisted of twenty volumes of text with fifteen hundred small plates bound in, plus twenty portfolios of unbound gravure plates. (These latter, larger plates are the ones from which the selection in this book has been made.) All in all, a total of approximately twenty-five hundred images—one of the largest photographic archives of this sort ever made by a single artist.

Issued in an edition limited to five hundred sets and priced at $3,000 per set, *The North American Indian* was aimed at museums, well-endowed libraries, and wealthy private collectors. More than three hundred of the sets were sold fairly quickly to such buyers.

And in those hands they vanished. They were not deliberately hidden; they were merely so large that they hid themselves. Automatically, they were placed in the Rare Book Rooms of the institutions which housed them, thus becoming invisible. Only rarely were they cross-indexed under Photography in card catalogues, for they were thought of more as ethnographic treatises than as photographic documents. Out of easy reach even for scholars, remote from the general public, they were easy to forget.

This was especially true since there was nothing to keep them in the public eye. Curtis never had another major exhibit of his work during his lifetime; indeed, it appears that there were no exhibits at all until the Morgan Library displayed part of its collection in 1971. (A second show, at the Witkin Gallery in New York City, followed closely in early 1972; now, of course, the deluge.) A few books on Indians were later published which included Curtis illustrations, but the reproductions were so poor as to convey nothing of the quality of his work. Since the gravure plates were not sold singly, only a few (from broken sets) circulated. Only one book about Curtis and his project has ever been written, but even in that monograph the reproductions were so poor as to make the author's claim for Curtis' stature seem incomprehensible.

Thus, while ironic, it is also understandable that the name of Edward S. Curtis appears in none of the major volumes of photographic history. After all, even his obituary in the New York Times mentioned his photographic work only once, in passing.

t would be natural to assume that the sudden current upsurge of interest in the photographs of Curtis is attributable primarily to the widespread "rediscovery" of American Indian culture which began in the middle 1960's. This new awareness, however, is neither the sole nor the prime cause of the Curtis revival. If it were, one would logically expect to see a similar, concurrent resurgence of interest in other photographers of Indians—William H. Jackson, Timothy O'Sullivan, F. A. Rinehart, and many more. But the work of these men has achieved no new prominence, and for good reason: the photographs of Edward S. Curtis are not only vastly different from, but far superior to, theirs on almost every count, and unless another unknown giant still lurks on the reserve shelves of some library The North American Indian will probably come to be recognized as the most profound document of pure Indian culture ever made.

To be sure, Curtis had several advantages over the photographers who preceded him in the nineteenth century. His equipment was somewhat more sophisticated than theirs had been (though that alone hardly accounts for the qualitative differences in the imagery of these men.) He had more time for—or, to be accurate, devoted more time to—studying his subject in the field. He had access to the work of his predecessors, so that he could learn from their limitations and oversights, and had access as well to a far larger body of historical and ethnographic information about the Indians than did any previous photographer. Furthermore, by the time Curtis began his work, at the turn of this century, the Indians had lost most of their "superstitious" (though hardly baseless) fears of having their spirits stolen by the camera's eye.

But these advantages were balanced by the many difficulties Curtis was forced to overcome. Unlike Jackson, O'Sullivan, and other early photographers, who encountered Indian culture when it was still vital and relatively untainted, Curtis had to deal with considerably modernized Indian nations and find ways to reconstruct the past therefrom. The title of one of his most moving images, that poignantly receding line of riders in "The Vanishing Race," (p. 53) expresses perfectly the tragedy of that stage in Indian history. The task he took upon himself—to explore and record every significant aspect of Indian life—was both more coherent and more demanding in its scope than anything attempted until then. And while the Indians had overcome some of their superstitions about photography, those had been replaced, quite sensibly, with suspicion of the motives of the photographers who persisted in streaming through their world and invading their privacy. Gaining—or, rather, regaining—their trust must be seen as one of Curtis' major accomplishments; exposure to the range of his imagery makes it obvious how intrinsic that trust was to his purpose.

It is that sense of purpose, more than anything else, which differentiates Curtis from all other photographers who have recorded the American Indian.* Jackson, O'Sullivan, and the rest were essentially documentarians, intent on capturing in photographs the visual facts, just the facts. Their images describe excellently in a scientific fashion, noting in a detached if accurate way the appearance of rituals, the details of costume, the distinctive physiognomical traits of assorted tribal representatives. These photographers—whose work, I should add, was and is still an invaluable part of the visual archives of Indian culture—functioned on a undeniably important but conceptually limited level.

urtis, in contrast, was intent on making not just images of but images about Indian life. He set out specifically and deliberately, to capture the spirit of the Indian lifestyle and invest his photographs with it. This goal, which he pursued with an almost fanatical selflessness—and which, as his results attest, he successfully achieved—is what distinguishes him from all who came before. Content with recording surfaces, others defined themselves implicitly as visual stenographers, while Curtis, insistent on rendering not only the surface but the substance, the very ethos of Indian life, became by virtue of that choice an interpreter of his subjects.

This may be taken as another way of saying that Curtis chose to function as an artist, but that word is semantically loaded and not necessarily significant in a response to photographic imagery. I use the word "interpreter" advisedly, then, to imply that Curtis imposed on his subject matter not only his own way of seeing (which all photographers impose) but also his personal, interior vision of what they were and what they symbolized.

Make no mistake about it: there may be such things as "objective" photographic documents, but Curtis' works are not among them. His body of imagery forms one man's intensely subjective record of his own responses to other people and their cultural matrix, an interpretative essay on an entire people and their way of life.

Because it does not pretend to objectivity, we tend naturally to question a work such as this. Are these actually photographs of the Indians, or indirect portraits of Curtis himself? Is the romanticism which resounds

*One photographer who must surely be excepted from this evaluation is Laura Gilpin, whose deeply committed studies of contemporary Indian life are truly a continuation of Curtis' labor of love.

throughout his work anything more than another white man's uncomprehending sentimentalization of an alien culture and philosophy? Can we, to get to the heart of the issue, trust Curtis' vision and accept what it reveals to us as true?

To answer this last question, we must come to terms with Curtis' style, his vision, and the relationships between them.

A glance through these images will indicate that Curtis was inarguably a stylist. His mastery of natural light as a modeling tool in the portraits, his unstrained but highly structured compositional sense, and his flair for recognizing instants of epiphany in his dramatic tableaux, all point to a highly developed and classically influenced way of seeing. Curtis knew how he wanted his photographs to look individually, and was obviously aware of the overall appearance of his total body of work as well. Certainly his alternation between hard and soft focus, always chosen to amplify the emotional content of the specific image, is also part of his style.

His vision—that is to say, his understanding of what he saw, above and beyond his way of seeing it—is unabashedly, even incurably, romantic. Webster defines romanticism as "signifying . . . the spirit of chivalry, adventure, and wonder, the preoccupation with picturesque and suggestive aspects of nature, and with the passionate in life." The work of Curtis could hardly be described better or more succinctly.

Since his style consistently echoes and reinforces his vision, Curtis' images are anything but accidental. Not only are they all carefully planned and previsualized, but, like pieces of a jigsaw puzzle, they are consciously designed to fit together in order to create the unity of that larger whole which is The North American Indian. And, because it is infused with that encompassing personal response to, and interpretation of, the subject, the work of Curtis must be seen as a simultaneous portrait and self-portrait, a blend of fact and feeling which demands a response as strong as the commitment which went into its making.

Why are we so willing to make this response? Why, when we know that romanticism of a different kind has distorted our perception of the Indian, are we able to trust these photographs, to certify a truth quotient in their message?

In the last analysis, it seems to me that we trust the images of Curtis because it is obvious from even one—any one—of the portraits that his subjects trusted him first and trusted him deeply, and that this trust was caver betrayed.

I suspect that they trusted him as they did not despite his romanticism but because of it; it was a match for their own. Pragmatic and unsentimental though it was, the Indian world view was also quintessentially romantic in the very best sense of the word, and the dictionary definition quoted above fits Curtis' subjects as closely as it fits the photographer himself. They were spokesmen for each other, Curtis and the Indians, and if these images are in one sense a self-portrait of Curtis they are also, in that same sense, the visual autobiography of Indian culture. The combined sensibilities of all participants in these photographic acts are merged in the resulting images.

Yes, the Indian vision of the universe was basically romantic, as was the cultural style and even the setting. One cannot easily determine where Curtis leaves off and the Indians begin, they are so entwined: look at "The Storm—Apache," (p. 137) "The Vanishing Race," (p. 53) and "The Apache Reaper" (p. 65). And his love for the shapes created by the interaction between the people and their land—another romantic trait—can be seen in such images as "A Mono Home," (p. 151) with its complex patterns of baskets, house, hills, and clouds.

Because Curtis was not imposing his romanticism on his subjects, but rather mirroring their own, he managed to keep his vision expansive and his way of seeing extraordinarily flexible. His images are always immediately recognizable, but they differ greatly from each other depending on the purpose they are intended to serve.

Without setting up rigid categories, I think it is illuminating to note that Curtis worked in several distinct veins, each of them exploring a different facet of the same culture.

One of these veins concentrates on the artifacts of Indian culture. These creations—baskets, costumes, weapons, tools—are treated by Curtis not simply as things but as manifestations of the Indian spirit. His photographs make them animate, and always reveal the beautifully functional shapes and textures of these works. It is significant, though, that no matter how remarkable it may be in its own right no artifact in any of Curtis' images is permitted to steal the scene from a human subject. Though the costume worn by "Wishham Girl" (p. 165) is stunning, Curtis relegates it to second place in the hierarchy of content—a stylistic decision which is also a philosophical stance.

Another of Curtis' interests was work—the tasks necessary to support life and the ways in which they were performed. Fishing, reaping, weaving, along with many other skills and crafts, were explored by Curtis in a way which recorded not only the significant tools and motions but also the spirit in which the work was done. "The Potter Mixing Clay," (p. 135) for example, is a powerful study which conveys not only the basic craft information but also the potter's own emotional connection with the earth and his own mortality, transmitting that to the viewer in a direct and deeply felt manner.

There are numerous other sub-genres (such as records of daily life) which will become apparent as one experiences these images again and again. Each serves to probe a specific area of Indian culture and is a variant—always with appropriate modifications—of Curtis' central style.

Two of these sub-genres, however, are particularly noteworthy in that they are the most emotionally charged sectors of the total document, the ones which would probably raise the most skepticism among ethnographers but which are nevertheless, for almost everyone who sees them, the most memorable: the portraits and the tableaux.

The portraits are, quite simply, superb. Compositionally, they have a classic purity and strength which seems ageless. Natural light is employed by Curtis in a consistently brilliant way to emphasize both obvious and subtle marks of character in a face, to establish the mood of each individual portrait, and to create an unusual feeling of space within a two-dimensional image.

In these portraits Curtis worked as a cartographer, reading each face as a map of the past and of the character of each sitter. Unlike other Indian photographers, who had photographed their subjects without attention to pose or environment, Curtis sought always to bring out the individual qualities of the men, women, and children before his lens. If his results are successful, and they are, we must recognize that Curtis' efforts were only half of what went into these images; the other half was the willingness of his sitters to reveal themselves with such grace and honesty.

As you go through the portraits, notice how Curtis resists the temptation to let artifacts distract him from the face itself—except in a few cases where some element of apparel is so strong a personal talisman that it is incorporated as part of the sitter's *persona*. Notice too how the people seem to *wear* the light as though it were a garment, or a second skin.

Most of all, notice the psychological nuances evoked in each image, and the wide range of such delicate inflections to which Curtis was sensitive. The fierce pride of "New Chest—Piegan" (p. 117) is not identical to that of "A Hopi Man," (p. 119) just as the wisdom on the face of "Red Cloud—Ogalala" (p. 169) differs from that of "Wife of Modoc Henry" (p. 25). These are portraits of absolutely individual and highly complex people, each of whom Curtis perceives as a unique being. Everything else about them is secondary to Curtis, and if they represent their culture in any way, they do so by their uniqueness rather than despite it.

As for the tableaux, such as "Cañon de Chelly—Navaho," (p. 9) and "The Three Chiefs—Piegan" (p. 175) . . . at times they seem like dreamscapes, so closely do they match all youthful fantasies of what life in the Old West was like. It is the heroic side of the Indian ethos which is dramatized in these photographs, but it would be a mistake to assume that, simply because there is a romantic streak therein, these images are not true to the texture of their lives. Brooding skies, sweeping vistas, snorting horses—the environment itself is romantic. How then could a people so attuned to the land not be romantic as well? Some of these scenes may have been staged, but Curtis was directing the original cast in its farewell performance, and theatrical events of that sort generate a special, magical truth all their own.

Edward Curtis covered all aspects of Indian life in great depth and with remarkable sensitivity to the connections between them, but the most remarkable segments of all are these portraits and tableaux. In them Curtis, like no other photographer before him, ambitiously attempted to record the spirit of a people, to show us all and to find out for himself what it felt like to be an Indian. These collaborations between Curtis and the Indians succeed because neither he nor they were exploiting each other, but were bent on the same goal.

It is to be regretted that Curtis finished his work before making movies in such locations became commonplace; his flair for the dramatic would have made him a marvelous filmmaker, and the Indians surely needed a spokesman in the early days of the film. Many of his images, in fact, seem like stills from a film, and if they are sometimes ambiguous—as is the mysterious "Waiting in the Forest—Cheyenne" (p. 51)—the basic message is nonetheless clear: Here was a great culture which had much to teach us, and we destroyed it. We do not deserve a document of that culture so clear, so profound, and so devoid of bitterness as this one, and yet we have it. To earn it, we must work to understand it. That labor begins with the realization that just as Edward Curtis stole the spirit of the Indians, they in turn stole his. Contemplate these photographs long enough and it may happen to you.

CURTIS: HIS LIFE

by T. C. McLuhan

Alone with my campfire, I gaze about on the completely circling hill-top, crested with countless campfires, around which are gathered the people of a dying race. The gloom of the approaching night wraps itself about me. I feel that the life of these children of nature is like the dying day drawing to its end; only off in the West is the glorious light of the setting sun, telling us, perhaps, of light after darkness.

E.S. Curtis,
1905.

At the age of 30, known to no one in the fields of either history or anthropology, and recognized only by a few for his photography, Edward Sheriff Curtis conceived his grandiose idea to produce an enduring and irrefutable record of the characteristics of the North American Indian and his surroundings. No history of the North American Indian founded upon the Indians' own words and aspiring to be the first photographic record of its kind had ever before been attempted. The task would require a prodigious amount of research, stamina, and labor.

Upon publication of the first two volumes of Curtis' *The North American Indian* in 1907–8, *The New York Herald* hailed it as "the most gigantic undertaking in the making of books since the King James edition of the Bible." Realizing the importance of the work and the magnitude of its intended scope, President Theodore Roosevelt was moved to write in his foreword to Volume One:

. . . Because of the singular combination of qualities with which he has been blest, and because of his extraordinary success in making and using his opportunities, [Mr. Curtis] has been able to do what no other man has ever done; what, as far as we can see, no other man could do. He is an artist who works out of doors and not in the closet. He is a close observer, whose qualities of mind and body fit him to make his observations out in the field, surrounded by the wild life he commemorates. He has lived on intimate terms with many different tribes of the mountains and the plains. He knows them as they hunt, as they travel, as they go about their various avocations on the march and in the camp. He knows their medicine men and their sorcerers, their chiefs and warriors, their young men and maidens. He has not only seen their vigorous outward existence, but has caught glimpses, such as few white men ever catch, into that strange spiritual and mental life of theirs; from whose inner most recesses all white men are forever barred. . . .

Edward Curtis was born near Whitewater, Wisconsin in 1868. In 1887, when he was 19, the family went West to the pioneer villages of Puget Sound. Shortly after their arrival his father, Johnson Curtis, who had hoped to find an easier life in Seattle, died of pneumonia and Edward and his brothers were faced with the support of the family.

At this time, Curtis was already proficient with a camera. His fascination with the lens of a stereopticon had led to the making of his own camera. The natural romance of Puget Sound—the mountains, the sea and the forest—provided stimulus and inspiration for his camera work, and his enthusiasm grew. New sights fired his imagination—the beauty of the natural harbors, the halibut schooners and fishing boats working in and out of port, the saw mills which covered the shores, the snow-crested mountains, and the Indian shacks cramped together along the shore at Seattle.

It was the Indians of Puget Sound, however, who interested him most. One of his earliest and most famous pictures was that of Princess Angeline (p. 17), daughter of Chief Seattle, who had surrendered his land (where Seattle now stands) to Governor Isaac Stevens in 1855. Curtis found Angeline living on the Seattle waterfront, and paying her a dollar he photographed her digging clams. Of his first Indian experiences Curtis recalled: "I made my first Indian photographs in 1896 on the shores of Puget Sound, spending part of two seasons in that field. Following that I spent a season with the Blackfoot Indians of Montana. A selection of photographs of the three seasons was sent to a National Photographic Exhibition where they won the grand prize." The winners, "The Mussel Gatherer" (p. 3) and "Homeward" (p. 157) then toured many foreign countries, gathering medals and praise.

Edward Curtis was also an ardent mountaineer and on one of his many ascents along the glaciers of Mount Rainier, complete with his 14 × 17 camera and glass negatives, he rescued a near-frozen party of climbers who had lost their way. It was a fortuitous event for Curtis. Three of the men in the group were to influence his life considerably—Dr. C. Hart Merriam, Chief of the U.S. Biological Survey; Gifford Pinchot, Chief of the U.S. Forestry Department; and George Bird Grinnell, editor of *Forest and Stream* magazine.

At the invitation of Merriam and Grinnell, Curtis joined his first major expedition. On May 30th, 1899, with a crew of 126, the steamship *Geo. W. Elder* sailed from Seattle for a two-month trek that would ultimately reach the Bering Sea. Some of the world's leading scientists were on board, including the naturalist John Muir and the ornithologist John Burroughs. There were two official photographers; Edward Curtis was one of them. The entire floating symposium was organized by E. H. Harriman, the wealthy railroad magnate. The main objective of the voyage was to explore the Alaskan waters of a route that had been mapped out beforehand. After a trip of nine thousand miles the party returned with five thousand pictures and over six hundred animal and plant species new to science. New glaciers were mapped and photographed and a new fjord 15 miles long was discovered. Curtis photographed many of the glaciers, but it was his Indian pictures on this trip which established his artistic genius.

It was an impressive experience for Curtis, which he later described as his "first contact with men of letters and millionaires." It was also the beginning of a thirty-year spiritual liaison between the photographer and the mysteries of Indian life.

t the turn of the century, the idea of a vanishing race had for most Americans romantic rather than realistic significance. Curtis' decision to record the beauty and strangeness of Indian life came at a decisive time. Realizing that the passing of every old man and woman meant the risk of losing forever the knowledge of sacred rites and traditions—that their world would disappear in death—Curtis burst into a fury of work.

In his desire to portray North American Indian life, Edward Curtis sought to create a living human document that would be both artistic and true to the subject matter, through his photographic lens and his recordings.

It was a period of painful transition for the Indians when Curtis began his work. The sacred lands of their ancestors had been overrun and the wild herds of the buffalo had disappeared. Hunting had given way to the digging of irrigation ditches. Red Cloud (p. 169) was almost 90, blind and dreaming of the days when his people were once monarchs of all they surveyed. Geronimo, (p. 173) 76 and subdued in spirit, was virtually a prisoner at Fort Sill, Oklahoma, growing watermelons and tending his small vegetable patch. Joseph, (p. 115) the last of the Nez Percé "non-treaty" Chiefs, had been confined to the Colville Reservation at Nespilim, Washington, when Curtis first made his acquaintance. In the summer following his death in September, 1904, Curtis returned to Nespilim to be present at the "Joseph Potlatch"—the giving away of all his earthly possessions.

Grinnell enthusiastically encouraged Curtis' interest in photographing Indian life and the following summer Curtis joined him in northern Montana, the home of the Blackfoot and Piegan tribes. Grinnell had already spent many seasons with them and had received the name "Fisher Hat."

Within ten days of witnessing the Blackfoot Sun Dance with Grinnell, Curtis was photographing the secret rites and rituals of the Hopi in southern Arizona. Difficulties in carrying out his field work had only just begun, lack of money being the most pressing one.

Throughout the rest of his 30 year effort the search for funds was to continue to be the major preoccupying problem for Curtis. For nine years he labored at his own expense. His photographic studio in Seattle was the subject of several mortgages, although financial stress was relieved for a little while when friends in Seattle succeeded in raising twenty thousand dollars. He worked obsessively, lecturing, writing, raising funds. He wrote a series of articles for Scribner's Magazine which appeared in 1906 and 1909 and brought him wide recognition. His series of exhibitions at the Waldorf-Astoria (March 1905) from his collection of Indian pictures earned him further acclaim, including the interest and patronage of Theodore Roosevelt. Post-cards of his Indian pictures were printed, announcements as to the progress of his work were distributed to friends and potential supporters, and Christmas notes were sent reminding people of his studio work in Seattle and suggesting the purchase of "Curt-tones"*, or "gold tones" as they were more popularly known.

In 1906, through Theodore Roosevelt, Curtis was introduced to J. Pierpont Morgan. Speaking of the meeting Curtis said: "The fate of the enterprise hinged on my first interview with J. Pierpont Morgan and the success of that interview was the basic factor in the completion of *The North American Indian*. More than half of the $1,500,000 cost involved in the undertaking was borne by Mr. Morgan and the Morgan estate." Initially, Morgan set up a fund of $75,000 for Curtis to use at the rate of $15,000 a year for the expenses of doing the field work. The loan was in the form of an advance subscription, and while it was not a salary it immediately released Curtis from much of the pressure of public-

ity work, so he could devote more time to his photography.

Plans were drawn up. *The North American Indian* would contain twenty volumes, each volume being complete in itself. The entire work would study the customs, ceremonials and daily life of the tribes west of the Mississippi from New Mexico to Alaska. It was an arduous task. Most of his photographic work was done before the days of the automobile. Cameras were cumbersome and heavy and all his pictures were taken on glass plates which were not only heavy but exceedingly difficult to care for and travel with. An enormous amount of equipment accompanied him on his journeys. Baggage included not only photographic equipment, but also his Edison recorder, a library of many volumes, tents, food, sometimes a Coleman gas stove (depending on the locale), bedding and all personal belongings for a group of three or four.

There were many heartbreaks and frustrations. On one occasion in southern Arizona, floods destroyed hundreds of his plates, wiping out months of valuable work. Curtis promptly started all over again. Edmond S. Meany, the Seattle historian, accompanied Curtis among the Sioux in the summer of 1906 on the northern plains of Dakota and sharply recalled some of the difficulties among the Ogalalas. "At dark a terrific storm struck the camp. The tent-poles broke and the tents flattened to the ground. Five Indian ponies in the neighborhood were killed by lightning. At another time the equipment wagon got stuck in the mud in the middle of the White River and had to be taken apart before it could be got out. To the traveller such experiences are not so serious as to the photographer, for the results of many months of hard work may be lost in a moment by a careless driver."

Oftimes Curtis' presence and intentions were not totally understood. He was shot at four times. He remarked on one such occasion: "I have grown so used to having people yell at me to keep out, and then punctuate their remarks with mud, rocks and clubs that I pay but little attention to them if I can only succeed in getting my picture before something hits me."

Remarkably intuitive and possessing a great understanding of the seemingly capricious and whimsical Indian character, Curtis was able through his quiet persistence to overcome the apprehension, deep-rooted suspicions and fears of the most reticent of chiefs. Through his lens he caught glimpses of their inner life which no other white man had approached, and unearthed material new to anthropologists. He celebrated life with the Indians and discussed with them their religious mysteries around the campfire whilst passing the pipe around, and the old men would say "He is just like us, he knows about the Great Mystery."* He cared.

In speaking of Curtis, Professor Meany once said that he had "met ethnologists, archaeologists, linguists, historians and artists, but none of them seemed to come so close to the Indian as he; so close that he seems a part of their life."

How did he do it? Speaking to a reporter of *The New York Times* in April, 1911, he stated: "Usually they know me beforehand. An agent has gone on ahead and explained everything, and they are expecting me. It is not always settled then, however. Frequently I have a lot of explaining to do. Sometimes I have been ordered peremptorily to leave the country. In such a case, it is a matter of using every wit you have to convince them that you ought to stay. On one occasion a child of whom I had taken a photograph fell and killed herself. I knew what they thought. I got out. I didn't wait for daylight either." On another

---

*Of this luminous finish, Curtis said: "The ordinary photographic print, however good, lacks depth and transparency, or more strictly speaking, translucency. We all know how beautiful are the stones and pebbles in the limpid brook of the forest where the water absorbs the blue of the sky and the green of the foliage, yet when we take the same iridescent pebbles from the water and dry them they are dull and lifeless. So it is with the orthodox photographic print, but in the Curt-tones all the translucency is retained and they are as full of life and sparkle." The gold-toning process was achieved by tinting the reverse side of the glass negative with a gold finish.

*Quoted in Meany Edmond S., "Hunting Indians with A Camera," from *World's Work*, March 1908.

occasion he related how another child had died while he was in the area. "He was ill when I got there; I didn't photograph him, but these unanswerable arguments didn't count at all. He had died while I was there, and I had to get out."

After work had been underway for 14 years, Curtis found many of the Indians not only willing but anxious to help. He explained that "the ordinary investigator going among them to secure information for a magazine article, they do not favor. But they have grasped the idea that this is to be a permanent memorial of their race, and it appeals to their imagination. Word passes from tribe to tribe about it. A tribe that I have visited and studied lets another tribe know that after the present generation has passed away men will know from this record what they were like, and what they did, and the second tribe doesn't want to be left out. Tribes that I won't reach for four or five years yet have sent me word asking me to come and see them . . . ."

"There was old Black Eagle," continued Curtis, "an Assiniboin, 90 years old, who had all his life refused to talk about his nation to white men. At last he became convinced that his tribe ought to get into the record, and he unbent, and gave me a great amount of valuable information."

It was not a matter of mere questioning for Curtis, but one of discussion, conversation and argument. "If I find a man who won't talk even after all this, I have a way which seldom fails," he said. "I begin talking to him about the religion of another tribe; or perhaps it is his own but I pretend that it is another. In the course of my talk I purposely make some theological error. It irritates him. 'Why, that isn't so,' he blurts out; and before he knows it he is telling me why it isn't so and going on to other points in his creed."

Months were spent beforehand in the study of a tribe's mythology and history and Curtis would avail himself of the advice and knowledge of leading scholars on the subject. Only when he felt sufficiently briefed did he begin the actual field work. It was not just a matter of going to one tribe and coming away with photographs and information. His first visit with the Hopis, for example, was in 1900, but he didn't complete and publish the work on them until 1922.

Initially Curtis thought that the project would take 15 years of his life. It consumed 30. Always, it demanded the same strenuous work schedule. In describing his work pattern for the material acquired amongst the Sioux, the Apsaroke and the Hidatsa, he wrote: "We closed the moving camp only when severe winter drove us from the field. Then another session of uninterrupted writing in a small log cabin in the mountains of Montana. There we settled down and took up work on Volumes III and IV.

"Our party consisted of four men. Breakfast hour was 7:30, beginning active work at 8:00, a half hour for lunch, an hour for supper, then working until 1:00 a.m. This was done every day of the month until spring. I did not take a day off during that time, the only interruption being a single trip to the post office, six miles away. I permitted mail to come to our camp but once a week and no newspapers were allowed. Every thought and every moment had to be given to the work."

It was the same routine with his work amongst the Arikara, Atsina, Cheyenne, Arapaho, Yakima, Klickitat and Kutenai. Reported Curtis: "In the early winter three of us hibernated in an isolated cabin on Puget Sound. Here we did the final work on Volumes, V, VI and some on VII—several months of incessant work of fifteen hours a day, again with but one mail a week and no newspapers. Mr. Myers and I took two Sundays a month off and visited our families; and during the winter we had but one visitor and he but for a few minutes. The long strain

of work here was such that I was seriously worn out toward the end and on the last week of the final reading and correcting of the manuscript, I could not leave my bed.*

ield work was facilitated by the efforts of a number of people, none of whom was more devoted than W. E. Myers. He spent nearly twenty years with Curtis and his assistance is acknowledged by Curtis in all but two of his volumes. Curtis described Myers as a "rapid shorthand writer and typist who had majored in English Literature. In spelling, he was a second Webster." But his most astonishing asset was his uncanny ear for phonetics, a fact which greatly enhanced the value of Curtis' work, one of the more valuable features being the inclusion of Indian vocabularies. Curtis relates how after spending an evening in an Indian camp listening to dance songs and upon returning to their own camp, "Myers would phonetically sing song after song he had heard, without the slightest understanding of what he was singing." He was also capable of repeating without hesitation a seven syllable word within seconds of hearing it from an old informant. His skill was "awesome magic" to the Indians.

Curtis also had the services of George Hunt as interpreter/informant amongst the Kwakiutl. Hunt was the son of a Scotch employee of the Hudson's Bay Company and a Tsimshian woman, and had lived his 60 years amongst the Kwakiutl. He was "possessed of an excellent memory," wrote Curtis, and "has so thoroughly learned the intricate ceremonial and shamanistic practices of these people, as well as their mythologic and economic lore, that today our best authority on the Kwakiutl Indians is this man, who, without a single day's schooling, minutely records Indian customs in the native language and translates it word by word into intelligible English." Hunt was also known for his valuable contribution to Dr. Franz Boas' work amongst the Kwakiutl.

A. B. Upshaw, an educated Apsaroke from the Carlisle Indian School, and son of Crazy Pend d'Oreille, proved to be of "inestimable value" to Curtis in collecting material from the Indians. In speaking of his Plains Indians work and crediting Upshaw with "getting [him] into the heart of the northern Plains Indian in a way that gave [him] the greatest satisfaction," Curtis wrote F. W. Hogge in August, 1908, and said of his Crow material: "I personally feel that it is a picture of Indian life closer than will often be reached by a white man."

Hunts To Die, a Mountain Crow, was another of Curtis' Indian informers to whom he felt much indebted. Born in 1838, Curtis described him as "a veteran of unusual mentality, from whom was obtained a large part of the information respecting the Apsaroke. . . . In early manhood he was a magnificent warrior who scarcely knew his physical limitations, but at thirty years of age he was so seriously wounded by a Sioux bullet as to be barred from further action on the field of battle, yet he lives to make this portion of the story of the Indian more closely portray the primitive life than has been possible in the preceding volumes of the series."

In the early years of his work, Curtis experienced difficulty in getting past Indian agents until he was provided with a letter of introduction from Commissioner Leupp, which granted him full freedom on all reser-

*Quoted in Andrews, Ralph W., *Curtis' Western Indians*. Bonanza Books, New York, pp 42–43.

vations, plus the cooperation of the Indian agents. U.S. Indian Commissioner Francis E. Leupp believed in what Curtis was doing: "Mr. Curtis' harvest has passed far beyond the statistical or encyclopaedic domain; he has actually reached the heart of the Indian; and has been able to look out upon the world through the Indian's own eyes. This gives us so vivid a color to his writing that his readers not only absorb but actually feel the knowledge he conveys. I do not think I exaggerate the facts in saying that the most truthful conceptions of the Indian race which will ever form themselves in the mind of posterity may be drawn from this great work."

It is fortunate that Curtis was imbued with such a sense of purpose. His biographical sketches of Indian chiefs and warriors, drawn firsthand, are rich in historical detail and represent the Indian point of view.

He also meticulously recorded the extensive story-telling at which the Indians were skilled, and these accounts provide important documentation of earlier days. Bull Chief, for example, was able to trace back Crow history through the lives of ten chiefs.

In an effort to relate the rhythms of their lives, Curtis worked diligently at putting the Indian verbal reminiscences to paper and recording their songs and ceremonials. To the Indian, Curtis and his modern equipment must have been viewed as part of the "wilds of civilization," the most startling example of this being his Edison wax-cylinder phonograph machine.

The incantations and songs were all recorded on wax rolls. The scores and words were then written from the wax rolls. "The singers and fellow tribesmen," said Curtis, "were awestruck on hearing the song as repeated from what they called 'the magic box.' The securing of . . . sacred songs was exceedingly difficult. All songs were considered as the personal property of the singer, and a part of his life. Many of them were ultra sacred. I must add that the song being the property of its originator was passed on to the oldest son and so passed on to their descendants."

In preparing for publication the songs given in the volumes, Mr. Edgar Fischer, who transcribed for Curtis much of the music both from his personal field notes and from the phonographic records made by other members of the party, explained that "the subject has been regarded from the viewpoint of the student of music rather than of the artist; that is to say, no attempt has been made, however interesting it might have been, to arrange the songs in conformity with the musical canons of the white man. The aim has been to record them, so far as this can be done in our musical notation, exactly as they are sung by the Indians, with regard to accent, rhythm, and metrical division, so that any one, reading them carefully, may be able to form an accurate idea of Indian music as it is actually rendered. . . . The earnest student will find in these songs a wealth of emotion and musical significance with which they will hardly be credited at first reading."

The hazards of recording were many. One had to worry about oiling the machine and protecting the wax records from dust and dirt and excessive heat and cold. Any undue friction would make a grind or rumble. The spring motor type, as his was, had to be fully wound at all times, or all harmony would be destroyed. The cylinder of this period was made of a light brown wax compound which if not given the utmost care would become pitted with molds and eventually petrify with age. In addition, the speaker or singer had to be within a certain distance of the horn and the intensity of the voice had to be carefully regulated. Yet despite the complexities of this task, it is reported that Curtis recorded over 10,000 songs, over 700 of which are still intact today at the University of Indiana.

Curtis was an enthusiast for his subject matter to the point of being a fanatic; he was also a perfectionist. Some of his pictures took years of planning to get just the right effect and point of view, a notable example being that of the "Three Chiefs" (p. 175)—Four Horns, Small Leggings and Mountain Chief, all old-time Blackfoot warriors, on the prairies of Montana, under a threatening sky. It cost Curtis the expense of three trips to get it. One trip was spent in locating a pool of water, and the other two in cultivating the chiefs.

He was equally careful of historical fact: "In my close personal study of the Little Big Horn battlefield (1905–1907) I took with me the three Crow scouts, White Man Runs Him, Goes Ahead, and Hairy Moccasins, who, with other scouts and Mitch Boyer, guided the command from the Yellowstone up the Rosebud and across from its waters to the Little Bighorn. These three men remained with Custer until he was actively engaged in the final brief fight. With these three scouts and Upshaw as interpreter, I travelled carefully time after time over all the ground covered by the troops in this encounter. I also visited the Sioux country and interviewed many participants. Red Hawk whose recollection of the fight seemed to be particularly clear, I persuaded to visit the field with me. His description of the battle was exceedingly lucid and remarkably detailed for one who had been a participant. I also went over the ground with Two Moons and a party of his Cheyenne warriors. Following this study I accompanied General Charles A. Woodruff, U.S.A., over the area covered by the troops. In this study we had with us the three Crows, as I particularly desired that the testimony of these men might be considered by an experienced army officer. Following the day spent on the field with General Woodruff and the scouts, I visited the country of the Arikara and interviewed the scouts of that tribe who had been with the command, gathering much valuable information from them." Curtis' version of the battlefield shows significant differences with the official version drawn in 1891 by R. B. Marshall.

n Curtis' quest for realism, there were many spell-binding adventures. He took direct part in the Hopi Snake Dance and of this experience he said: "I participated in that nine day and night ceremony. I fasted through the nine days; also, as prescribed by Hopi priests I had no contact with members of my party and followed the rules of celibacy. Dressed in a G string and snake dance costume and with the regulation snake in my mouth I went through the . . . dance." The opportunity enabled him to obtain some unique photographs of the occasion—among them the Snake and Antelope dancers (p. 73). Initiation into the secret orders, however, was not an unmixed delight. Curtis described his feelings after another nine day and night ceremony in the desert of Arizona. "I left them at dawn on the last day [and] if any one had tried to pick up my trail he would have found it forty feet wide, though I was trying to walk a straight line. Dancing, fasting, and all the rest of it, it was not easy."

His wish to "touch nature" with his camera took him down the Colorado River on the steamship *Iola*, in search of material; but most of the trip was spent in rescuing the boat from sand bars and rocks. Fording rivers in his canvas covered, steel-spring wagon became commonplace. Tremendous strength and endurance were required. Frontier life was exhilarating but it had its consequences. Curtis' health suffered

from overwork. Family life was neglected by the long absences. Whenever it was at all feasible, his wife, Clara, and their four children would accompany him, sometimes together, other times in turn, but it was a strain for everyone, which ultimately led to divorce. Curtis was obliged to leave Seattle and took up headquarters in Los Angeles. His wife was granted legal possession of his work.

1913 brought the sudden death of Mr. Morgan. Curtis' financial drama was never-ending: "I was in New York at the time and at once began an up-to-date financial report on our situation and account of the project which I delivered to the auditors of the Morgan bank. Some time later, I received a call from the bank, saying Mr. Morgan's son would like to see me. The following day I made my call. I was literally numb with apprehension, knowing that practically all of the elder Morgan's explorations in foreign lands had been closed by cable; also I knew that all commitments for purchases of art objects and paintings had been cancelled, and that a great part of his paintings were being sold. Considering all this, I could not see how the North American Indian project could be continued.

"Mr. Morgan's greeting was decidedly cordial; his handsclasp gave me hope. Without preliminaries he began the discussion of the Indian work, stating, 'I can well understand your anxiety as to what's to be done about *The North American Indian*. As a family, we have discussed the matter thoroughly and have decided to finish the undertaking as Father had in mind. We know that's what Father would want us to do.' He then outlined the plans he had in mind. We would discontinue all sales efforts and devote all energy and money to the completion of the field work and publication. The sales office on Fifth Avenue was to be closed and all business matters handled from the Morgan bank.

"I was to plan my field season and text work so that I could spend a few winter weeks in New York, each year. I at once mapped out plans for the field work to complete the twenty volumes. I wrote Myers of the plans and locations of our coming seasons research. We were to start the season among the Mandans and Arikara on the upper Missouri River."

urtis visited more than eighty tribes and took over 40,000 photographs. Why he chose to photograph some and not others was sometimes a question of the picturesque. The Wishham he found "refreshing" and "radically different" from any other tribe he had seen to date. He was enchanted by their high prowed canoes, wealth of beliefs in magic and the widespread practice of tattooing by both sexes. The Havasupai provided him with "the most unique homeland of any tribe." In the Cataract Cañon, a branch of the Grand Cañon of the Colorado, it "is but a tiny garden spot in a vast chaotic wilderness," wrote Curtis. To reach their home was no small feat. "One must first make the trip across the plateau," he continued, "to the rim of the cañon, no small feat, and then he who would enter must take his choice of two trails; either one will try the courage of all but the experienced traveller of cañon trails. . . . As our pack animals picked their way down the trail and entered this cañon home, the peach trees were in bloom, birds were singing, all in the joy of life and spring. I could but think, 'This is paradise'."

Curtis never once lost sight of his goal. In the face of criticism he

remained unyielding and determined. There were many academic arguments to deal with. Some centered around the title presentations of his pictures; others concerned themselves with the manner in which his subjects were dressed. It is a fact that while among the tribes of the Pacific Northwest he carried with him a bag of wigs and a good supply of primitive garments. He explains in his writings that the woven cedar bark capes were prepared especially for him by the Kwakiutl men and women. The furs and capes that appear in some of his photographs from this region had not been worn for years. Curtis wanted to capture more of the past than was there. Hair was worn short when he was there, so he had the natives don his wigs, which were legitimate representations of the earlier hair styles. The practice of wearing abalone shells as nose rings had entirely disappeared. Yet in some of his pictures of this region, Curtis was able to persuade the natives to wear them for the occasion. The abalone shells were at one time the most valued ornaments of the wealthy class.

In 1927, Curtis took his last field trip to the Arctic gathering data and photographs for *The North American Indian*. It was not unlike his first visit with Merriam and Grinnell in 1899 when, in a canoe at the face of the Muir Glacier, he had taken photographs for the Harriman Alaska Expedition. A craft named the *Jewel Guard* was purchased at Nome which Curtis described as "an ideal craft for muskrat hunting in the swamps but certainly never designed for storms in the Arctic Ocean." Upon reaching Little Diomede Island they were hit by a storm which "came from all the four points of the compass. For four days and nights, we swung hither and yon on our chain tether. As we swung shoreward, we could almost touch the rock cliff which towered hundreds of feet skyward; the ground swells lifted us high in the air and dropped us with such force that it seemed beyond belief that our wooden craft would not be split asunder. . . ." Everyone emerged unharmed.

he twenty volumes of *The North American Indian* were under the editorial management of Mr. Frederick Webb Hodge, in charge of the Bureau of Ethnology Smithsonian Institution, and editor of the *American Anthropologist*. One of his comments to Curtis was: "From the artistic point of view, there are others far more competent to judge than I; yet I doubt if anyone has derived greater inspiration and delight or has been more completely transported to the Mesa country of the Southwest during the short periods that I have been able to study these marvelous productions. Nevertheless, it is the ethnologic and historical side that most strongly appeals to me, not because I have travelled and lived with some of your subjects, but because of the knowledge that you are making a lasting record of a dying race—a record that, less than a generation hence, must prove to be priceless to those who would know what has gone before."

Each volume contains its own appendix which summarizes the tribes therein, covering the areas of language, population, dress, dwellings, primitive foods, arts and industries, games, political organization, social organization, marriage, culture hero, ceremonies, medicine men, burial customs, vocabularies, biographical sketches, winter count, and music. The volumes of text are accompanied by twenty corresponding portfolios. Each volume consists of about 300 pages, and there are 1,500 photogravure prints in the text volumes. Each portfolio consists of 36 or more copperplate photogravures, measuring 12 × 16 inches, on 18 × 22 sheets, the total for the portfolios being 722 plates. The photogravures were by John Andrew & Son, Boston and the Suffolk Engraving Co., Cambridge. The publishers were The University Press: Cambridge (volumes 1—5) and The Plimpton Press: Norwood, Mass. (volumes 6—20). A great deal of time and energy was expended in the choosing of paper and the determination of printing and binding techniques. Materials were chosen for their enduring qualities. The entire work was printed on imported hand-made paper of the highest grade. A Holland paper of a rich tone was used for the volumes, and a separate and special Japan vellum was selected for the portfolios. The *New York Herald*, June 16th, 1907, estimated that the cost of the photogravures and illustrations alone would be $600,000, and added to that was another $250,000 for field expenses. Binding was three-quarter Levant (irregularly grained morocco leather) which added a further $300,000 to the total cost. Nothing was spared in order to make *The North American Indian* beautiful and lasting. It stands today, as it did then, as one of the finest, costliest and most exceptional examples of bookmaking and binding. It is a small wonder that this limited edition of 500 sets sold for between $3,000 and $3,850. A set today sells for $80,000.

Curtis' obsession with the urgent need to portray the Indian spirit and to dispel popular but false notions of Indian life, produced, apart from his field writings and pictures, an extraordinary film, an Indian opera, and two best sellers. The film, *In the Land of the Head Hunters*, was presented for the first time in 1914. It was the dramatization of primitive life on the shores of the North Pacific and was made during Curtis' three seasons with the Kwakiutl. The theater circular at that time descibed it as "every participant an Indian and every incident true to native life." It is said that the Kuwakiutl natives did all they could to help Curtis with his film. House fronts and totem poles were erected, dances and rituals were reproduced, canoes were tipped over in rough waters and the burning of a village was staged. Curtis even went so far as to pay the natives fifty cents each to shave off their mustaches for the film. It was his intention to reproduce an earlier period. Music drawn from the phonographic records of Indian music obtained in the field was composed by John J. Braham and played by a full orchestra. The film was greeted enthusiastically. Today the only existing copy of the original is located in Seattle.

On November 16th, 1911, the *New York Herald* reported that Curtis' first "Indian Picture Opera [was] applauded by an audience that filled the hall," referring to its opening at Carnegie Hall. It took the form of a running narrative with motion pictures and music to represent the story of a "vanishing race". The music was composed by Henry F. Gilbert (who had transcribed for Curtis many of the phonographic records of Indian songs) and played by a specially trained orchestra of twenty-two musicians. There reached a point where Curtis' novelties were the highlight of the New York and Washington theater season. His two best sellers—*Indian Days of Long Ago*, N.Y. World Book Co., 1914, and *Land of the Head Hunters*, N.Y. World Book Co.,1915—increased his popularity. Both were about Indian legends and folklore. His photographs, also, were often used to illustrate the books and articles of the day.

Curtis managed to preserve the beauty and pathos of Indian life. Many of his photographs have the qualities one finds in paintings —"qualities," said Dr. Chas. M. Kurt, Director of the Buffalo Fine Arts Academy in 1908, "obtainable only by the artist educated in composition, in the management of light and shadow masses, and the subordination of undue detail when the spirit of the work demands it—combined with the skill of the competent photographer knowing all that one should know concerning necessary periods of exposure under different light effects, the secrets of the development of negatives to produce results most desirable, and a knowledge of making prints that are in the highest degree artistic." He possessed the conscience of a scholar, but never got beyond grade school. His descriptions of some of the Northwest Coast ceremonials are regarded as among the best and most accurate available. Curtis was not without his predecessors—Henry Rowe Schoolcraft, T. L. McKenney and James Hall, and George Catlin, but in terms of the geographical area he covered and in the spaciousness of his narrative, he surpassed the work of these men.

If Curtis had any doubts as to the value of his work, one need only quote W. H. Holmes, Chief of the Bureau of American Ethnology. In speaking of its value for posterity he said: "The ordinary book of today will last but a few generations. This publication should last for a thousand years, and it would not be the part of wisdom to undertake the expenditure required for its issue without having a series of types satisfactory artistically and covering the ground ethnologically. . . . The project is a splendid one, and has an importance that can be realized only by those who having a true conception of the work proposed, take the trouble to assume the point of view of the student of human history a thousand years in the future."

Curtis summed up some of his own feelings in the first volume of his work: "The task has not been an easy one, for although lightened at times by the readiness of the Indians to impart their knowledge, it more often required days and weeks of patient endeavor before my assistants and I succeeded in overcoming the deep-rooted superstition, conservatism and secretiveness so characteristic of primitive people, who are ever loathe to afford a glimpse of their inner life to those who are not of their own. Once the confidence of the Indians was gained, the way led gradually through the difficulties, but long and serious study was necessary before knowledge of the esoteric rites and ceremonies could be gleaned. . . .

"It is . . . near to Nature that much of the life of the Indian still is; hence its story, rather than being replete with statistics of commercial conquests, is a record of the Indian's relations with and his dependence on the phenomena of the universe—the trees, and shrubs, the sun and stars, the lightning and rain—for these to him are animate creatures. . . '"

Edward Sheriff Curtis died on October 21st, 1952, in Los Angeles, at the age of 84 years. Through his portraiture of North American Indian life, he built a loving monument, which is both memorable and poetic.

LEGEND

The following descriptive material reflects Edward Curtis' own personal impressions of the event photographed and/or the feeling which each is meant to evoke. In some instances these notes have been taken from Curtis' field records, in others from his annotations of specific pictures, and in still others from a combination of both.

Page 1 **TRAVAUX—PIEGAN**

With most of the plains tribes the travois was the universal vehicle for transporting camp equipment, but is now rarely seen. In the days before the acquisition of horses a smaller form of the same device was drawn by dogs. The occasion of this picture was the bringing of the sacred tongues to the medicine-lodge ceremony.

Page 3 **THE MUSSEL GATHERER—SALISH**

Besides fish the most abundant sea foods are clams, mussels, oysters, crabs, sea-urchins, and sea-cucumbers. Of these the various species of clams are in greatest demand and they are eaten raw, steam-cooked, or steam-cooked and dried in smoke and then eaten so or boiled. Cuttelfish is a delicacy highly prized, and roasted sea-urchins were considered the most palatable food a wealthy chief could serve at his feast.

The primitive knives were slivers of flakable stone or large, sharpened mussel-shells.

Page 5 **THE RUSH GATHERER—KUTENAI**

Rushes gathered in the swamps and in the shallows of the lakes were dried and strung together into mats, which primitively were used for lodge-covers, mattresses, canoe cushions, and for a variety of domestic purposes.

Page 7 **THE BLANKET WEAVER—NAVAHO**

In Navaho-land blanket looms are in evidence everywhere. In the winter months they are set up in the *hogans*, but during the summer they are erected outdoors under an improved shelter, or as in this case, beneath a tree. The simplicity of the loom and its product are here clearly shown, pictured in the early morning light under a large cottonwood.

The Navaho are known the world over for their skill in weaving. Practically every Navaho woman is a weaver, and the blanketry produced is one of the most important handicrafts of any tribe of North American Indians. The greater portion of the wool from their hundreds of thousands of sheep is used in weaving, and in addition a considerable quantity of commercial yarn is employed for the same purpose. The Navaho woman weaves her blanket not so much for profit as for love of work. It is her recreation, her means of expressing imagination and her skill in execution.

Page 9 **CAÑON DE CHELLY—NAVAHO**

A wonderfully scenic spot is this in northeastern Arizona, in the heart of Navaho country—one of their strongholds, in fact. Cañon de Chelly exhibits evidences of having been occupied by a considerable number of people in former times, as in every niche at every side are seen the cliff-perched ruins of former villages.

In Cañon de Chelly, which may be termed the garden spot of the reservation, there are diminutive farms and splendid peach orchards irrigated with freshet water.

Page 11 **FOR A WINTER CAMPAIGN—APSAROKE**

It was not uncommon for Apsaroke war parties, mounted or afoot, to move against the enemy in the depth of winter. The warrior at the left wears the hooded overcoat of heavy blanket material that was generally adopted by the Apsaroke after the arrival of traders among them. The picture was made in a narrow valley among the Pryor mountains, Montana.

Page 13 **KWAKIUTL HOUSE-FRAME**

The two long beams in the middle are twin ridge-timbers, which are supported in the rear, as in the front, by a transverse beam resting on two uprights. At the extreme right and left are the eaves-timbers. The longitudinal and circular flutes of the columns are laboriously produced by means of a small hand-adze of primitive form. This frame is at the village Memkumlis.

Page 15 **KOTSUIS AND HOHHUQ—NAKOAKTOK**

These two masked performers in the winter dance represent huge, mythical birds. Kotsuis . . . and Hohhuq are servitors in the house of the man-eating monster Pahpaqalanohsiwi. The mandibles of these tremendous wooden masks are controlled by strings.

Page 17 **PRINCESS ANGELINE**

This aged woman, daughter of the chief Seattle, was for many years a familiar figure in the streets of Seattle.

Page 19 **APIO-MITA ("WHITE DOG")—BLOOD**

Page 21 **WAÍHUSIWA, A ZUÑI KYÁQǏMÂSSI**

Kyáqǐ-mâssi ("house chief") is the title of the Shíwanni of the north, the most important of all Zuñi priests. Waíhusiwa in his youth spent the summer and fall of 1866 in the East with Frank Hamilton Cushing, and was the narrator of much of the lore published in Cushing's Zuñi Folk Tales. A highly spiritual man, he is one of the most steadfast of the Zuñi priests in upholding the traditions of the native religion.

page 23 **QAHÁTǏKA GIRL**

A type of the desert Indian. They [the Qahátǐka] still depend mainly upon the natural food supply, such as mesquite pods and cactus fruit. One cannot help wondering how these Indians would have managed if Nature had made the giant cactus with a solid trunk. Here at the rock-strewn foot of the desert mountain, where scarcely any other form of vegetal life seems able to exist, provident Nature permits this variety of cactus to flourish, and to furnish unlimited quantities of food as well as material for the building of habitable houses.

Page 25 **WIFE OF MODOC HENRY—KLAMATH**

Page 27 **HLEÁSTǓNǓH—SKOKOMISH**

Generations of canoe life developed a people peculiarly strong of chest and shoulders, but squat in stature: a type not particularly prepossessing.

Page 29 **THE OLD CHEYENNE**

The Cheyenne retain no tradition of the houses of logs and earth which they doubtless used before emerging on the prairies. In the earliest times within the tribal recollection the tipi covering was of buffalo skins with the hairy side out, and not sewn permanently together, since they were transported by dogs. After horses were acquired the tipi became larger, requiring from ten to twenty-two poles and eighteen to twenty-two skins, which were dressed on both sides.

Page 31 **OGALALA WOMAN**

A face so strong that it is almost masculine, showing strikingly how slight may be the difference between the male and female physiognomy in some primitive people.

Page 33 **PORCUPINE—CHEYENNE**

At the summer gatherings for such occasions as the Sun Dance, the men sometimes protect their heads from the merciless sun by a thatch of cottonwood leaves.

Page 35 **BLACK BELLY—CHEYENNE**

The extreme age of this Cheyenne is quite apparent.

Page 37 **CHEYENNE GIRL**

Page 39 **THE WHALER**

A feat so remarkable as the killing of a whale with the means possessed by primitive men is inexplicable to the Indian except on the ground that the hunter has the active assistance of a supernatural being. Therefore the whaler and his wife observe a long and exacting course of purification, which includes sexual continence and morning and evening baths at frequent intervals from October until the end of the whaling season, which begins in May and ends about the last of June. Prayers and numerous songs form a part of every whaler's ritual. The secrets of their profession are handed down from father to son. . . .

The most successful whalers are those who, even though they inherited the profession, have found an object which represents the supernatural whale. This object is either a double-headed, black worm eleven inches long and an inch and a half thick, or a certain species of crab. Seeing either of these creatures, a man must throw his spear at it. If it be the worm, he takes it up and preserves it as a charm; if the crab, he removes the right claw and the breast of the shell.

Page 41 **THE WHALER—MAKAH**

Note the great size of the harpoon-shaft. Indian whalers implanted the harpoon-point by thrusting, not by hurling, the weapon.

Page 43 **NOOTKA METHOD OF SPEARING**

The harpoon for seals, porpoises, and salmon is double-headed so that if the point on the main shaft glances off, the other may perhaps lodge in the hunter's prey.

Page 45 **A NAKOAKTOK CHIEF'S DAUGHTER**

When the head chief of the Nakoaktok holds a potlatch (a ceremonial distribution of property to all the people), his eldest daughter is thus enthroned, symbolically supported on the heads of her slaves.

Page 47 **HESQUIAT ROOT DIGGER**

Nootka women very commonly wore the bark cape folded over the head, to protect the forehead from the tump-line, when carrying the burden-basket. The proper use of the cape was to shed the rain.

Page 49 **A HEAVY LOAD—SIOUX**

Summer and winter the Sioux woman performed the heavy work of the camp and what was seemingly drudgery was to her a part of the pleasure of life.

Page 51 **WAITING IN THE FOREST—CHEYENNE**

At dusk in the neighborhood of the large encampments young men, closely wrapped in non-committal blankets or white cotton sheets, may be seen gliding about the tipis or standing motionless in the shadow of the trees, each one alert for the opportunity to steal a meeting with his sweetheart.

Page 53 **THE VANISHING RACE—NAVAHO**

The thought which this picture is meant to convey is that the Indians as a race, already shorn of their tribal strength and stripped of their primitive dress, are passing into the darkness of an unknown future. Feeling that the picture expresses so much of the thought that inspired the entire work, [I have] chosen it as the first of the series.

Page 55 **A MOUNTAIN FASTNESS—APSAROKE**

The Apsaroke lived much among the mountains and nowhere do they seem more at home than on the streams and in the cañons of their forested ranges. A powerful tribe of mountaineers, subsisting entirely by the chase and quite independent of the uncertainties of agriculture, the Apsaroke regarded with more or less disdain their sedentary Hidatsa cousins, who tilled the soil and lacked the strength to carry on extensive predatory warfare. . . . While nearly all the wandering tribes frowned on agriculture, the Apsaroke seem to have been particularly averse to it.

Page 57 **BASKET MAKER—SKOKOMISH**

Basketry continues to be an important industry of many Puget Sound tribes, the bulk of the product passing into the hands of the dealers. . . . The numerous shapes and sizes of baskets fall into three divisions: the firm, frequently water-tight utensil of cedar- or spruce-root coils; the thin, flexible, imbricated receptacles used for storing personal possessions; and the open-meshed, checker-work baskets used for washing clams and for bearing burdens on the back.

Page 59 **POMO SEED-GATHERING UTENSILS**

The group includes a tight-mesh burden-basket for seeds, an open-mesh burden-basket for acorns and other nuts, two winnowing trays, and a seed-beater with which the seeds are brushed from the plant into the burden-basket.

Page 61 **A FEAST DAY AT ACOMA**

Franciscan missionaries early in the seventeenth century introduced certain public Christian rites among the Pueblos, which ever since have been performed, with an intermingling of native ceremonial practices, especially on the days of the saints to whose protection the villages were respectively assigned. The day of San Estevan, patron saint of Acoma, is September second.

Page 63 **WASHING WHEAT—SAN JUAN**

Threshed by the aid of animals and winnowed by tossing in the breeze, wheat is placed in loose-mesh baskets and submerged in the water of an acequia. Particles of earth are thus dissolved and floating bits of straw and chaff are scooped off. After thoroughly drying in the sun, the grain is stored in bags.

Page 65 **THE APACHE REAPER**

Here the Apache woman is seen in her small wheatfield harvesting the grain with a hand sickle, the method now common to all Indians of the Southwest.

Contrary to the general opinion, the Apache is a good worker. Men and women alike work at the heaviest sort of labor. The first Apache women I met were at work in a woods felling timber and cutting it into cordwood. To see women in the forest working as woodmen was a novel sight to me.

Page 67 **WALPI**

Picturesque Walpi, perched on the point of a rocky island in a sea of sand, is an irregular, rambling community-house built without design, added to in haphazard fashion as need arose; yet it constitutes a perfectly satisfying artistic whole.

Page 69 **A LOAD OF FUEL—ZUÑI**

The Zuñi tribe, now numbering twenty-two hundred, has been concentrated in the present pueblo and its farming villages for nearly two and a half centuries, and in the same valley for hundreds of years before. Only a people as frugal as all the pueblos in the use of fuel could still have an available supply in a region so poorly provided by Nature.

Page 71 **A CORNER OF ZUÑI**

The chamber at the left, with ladder-poles projecting from the hatch-way is the kiva of the north. Many dances are performed in the small plaza here shown. The dark material piled against one of the houses is sheep-dung for firing pottery.

Page 73 **ANTELOPES AND SNAKES AT ORAIBI**

The Antelope fraternity, at the right, and the Snake fraternity facing them at the left, engage in singing prior to handling the reptiles in the Snake dance. At the extreme right is the *kisi*, a cottonwood booth in which sits the custodian of the snake-jars, ready to hand out the reptiles one by one to the dancers.

Page 75 **ZUÑI GIRLS AT THE RIVER**

Page 77 **A HOPI GIRL**

Soft, regular features are characteristic of Hopi young women, and no small part of a mother's time used to be devoted to dressing the hair of her unmarried daughters. The original style is rapidly being abandoned, and the native one-piece dress here illustrated is seldom seen even at the less advanced of the Hopi pueblos.

Page 79 **WATCHING THE DANCERS**

A group of girls on the topmost roof of Walpi, looking down into the plaza.

Page 81 **ANDRÉS CAÑON**

Near Andrés cañon, south of Palm Springs, was Páinik, the winter residence of a branch of the Palm Cañon Cahuilla.

Page 83 **AN APACHE BABE**

A fortunate child picture giving a good idea of the happy disposition of Indian children, and at the same time showing the baby carrier or holder.

Page 85 **GETTING WATER—APACHE**

A picture made in early spring on the banks of White River, Arizona. The water bottle is the typical Apache one of basketry covered with piñon gum.

Page 87 **APACHE-LAND**

Apache horsewomen in a small valley of the White Mountain region. The horses are laden with the complete camp equipage, on top of which the women have taken their seats.

At the present, the greater part of the Apache reside on the White Mountain reservation, Arizona, comprising more than 3,500,000 acres, with agency headquarters at Whiteriver and San Carlos. This reservation is part of the great tableland of southeastern Arizona, being a succession of mountains and high, park-like mesas, broken here and there with valleys and watered by limpid streams. The highlands are wooded with pine, cedar, fir, juniper, oak, and other trees, while in the valleys are mistletoe-laden cottonwood as well as willow, alder, and walnut, which, with smaller growth, are interwoven with vines of grape, hop, and columbine, in places forming a veritable jungle. On every hand, whether on mountain or in valley, many varieties of cactus grow in profusion; and in springtime cañon and vale, mountain-side and mesa, are all aglow with wild flowers.

Page 89 **AS IT WAS IN THE OLD DAYS**

In early days, before white men invaded the Great Plains and ruthlessly slaughtered them by hundreds of thousands, bison were of prime importance to the hunting tribes of the vast region in which those animals had their range. The bison was not only the chief source of food of the Plains Indians, but its skin was made into clothing, shields, packs, bags, snowshoes, and tent and boat covers; the horns were fashioned into spoons and drinking vessels; the sinew supplied thread for sewing, bow strings, and fibre for ropes; the hair was woven into reatas, belts, personal ornaments, and the covers of sacred bundles; and the dried droppings, "buffalo-chips," were used as fuel. So dependent on the buffalo were these Indians that it became sacred to them, and many were the ceremonies performed for the purpose of promoting the increase of the herds.

Page 91 **HUPA TROUT TRAP**

Only one form of fish-trap was used. This was a receptacle of poles and withes, about ten feet long and four feet wide, which was placed in a riffle below the weir, with the floor of the middle section raised slightly above the surface of the water. Salmon on striking the weir would turn back, and those that entered the trap quickly found themselves carried by the current and their own momentum into the lower end of the trap, whence they were unable to escape. This device was placed also at the downstream angle of two converging lines of fence, one of which extended quite to the bank, while the other left a channel around its upper end. Salmon swimming through this passage were driven back into the triangular area between the two wings, and so down into the trap. Trout were also caught in similar fashion but bone hooks, and dipnets suspended on triangular frames of stocks, were more commonly used.

Page 93 **CANOE OF TULES—POMO**

In an emergency a craft even more simple than this was made by fashioning a long bundle of tules, which the boatman rode astride with his legs in the water.

Page 95 **ON SPOKANE RIVER**

Spokane river, from a short distance below its head in Coeur d'Alêne lake to its confluence with the Columbia, flows through the midst of what was the territory of the Spokan Indians. The character of the country through which the stream passes for some miles above its mouth is well shown in the picture. Northward from the stream lie the mountains among which the three Spokan tribes hunted deer and gathered berries, and southward stretch the undulating plains where they obtained their supplies of roots.

Page 97 **PIMA KI**

The old-time round dwelling of the Piman tribes. In construction it was much the same as the earth lodge of the tribes of the northern plains, the chief difference lying in the fact that its top is practically flat and is not provided with an opening for the escape of smoke, as well as in the lack of an extended or built-out entrance way. The *ki* was usually about 15 feet in diameter. As the winter climate of southern Arizona is very mild, only a small fire was needed to keep the *ki* warm in even the coldest weather, the smoke from which became absorbed in part by the earthen roof, or escaped through the doorway.

Page 99 **ASSINBOIN MOTHER AND CHILD**

Page 101 **WINTER—APSAROKE**

In the thick forests along the banks of mountain streams the Apsaroke made their winter camps. The country which the Apsaroke ranged and claimed as their own was . . . extensive. . . . In area it may be compared, east and west, to the distance from Boston to Buffalo, and north to south, from Montreal to Washington—certainly a vast region to be dominated by a tribe never numbering more than fifteen hundred warriors. The borders of their range were, roughly, a line extending from the mouth of the Yellowstone southward through the Black Hills, thence westward to the crest of the Wind River mountains, north-westward through the Yellowstone Park to the site of Helena, thence to the junction of the Musselshell and the Missouri, and down the veritable Eden of the Northwest. With beautiful broad valleys and abundant woods, no part of the country was more favorable for buffalo, while its wild forested mountains made it almost unequalled for elk and other highland game.

page 103 **ATSINA WARRIORS**

Page 105 **ON THE LITTLE BIG HORN—APSAROKE**

This picturesque camp of the Apsaroke was on the Little Bighorn river, Montana, a short distance below where the Custer fight occurred.

In stature and vigor the Apsaroke excelled all other tribes of the Rocky Mountain region, and were surpassed by none in bravery and in devotion to the supernatural forces that gave them strength against their enemies.

Page 107 **FISHING CAMP—LAKE POMO**

Large quantities of a species locally called black-fish are still taken annually by the Lake Pomo. The fish are split down the back, and after the removal of backbone, head, and entrails, are hung on pole racks to dry in the sun for about two weeks, after which they are thoroughly cured in smoke-houses. Tule huts are not now seen, the one here shown having been built especially for the occasion.

Page 109 **ASSINIBOIN HUNTER**

The Assiniboin belong to the Siouan stock. The popular name of this tribe is a Chippewa appellation signifying "stone cookers," referring doubtless to the custom of boiling meat with hot stones in bark vessels.

Important game animals were moose, mule deer, white-tail deer, woodland caribou, elk and bear. The art of snaring moose with rawhide ropes suspended in their trails was learned from the Shuswap. In stalking this animal the hunter of today is exceptionally wary. When the moose bolts at an unavoidable sound, if it happens to run against the wind, the hunter can only follow and start it up again. When it runs across the wind, he lies in ambush a few hundred yards on the lee side of its track, knowing that the moose will soon swerve back to run with the wind; and with good luck the animal will pass within shooting distance. From time to time moose used to become very abundant, then an epidemic would reduce their numbers.

Page 111 **THE OFFERING—SAN ILDEFONSO**

A pinch of cornmeal tossed into the air as an offering to the numerous deities of the Tewa, but especially to the sun, is a formality that begins the day and precedes innumerable acts of the most commonplace nature.

Page 113 **NEZ PERCÉ BABE**

The Nez Percé began his preparation for spiritual attainment almost in infancy. The child, either boy or girl, when less than ten years of age was told by the father or the mother that it was time to have *tiwatitmas*—spiritual power. "This afternoon you must go to yonder mountain and fast. When you reach the place of fasting, build a fire and do not let it die. As the Sun goes down, sit on the rocks facing him, watch while he goes from sight, and look in that direction all night. When the dawn comes, go to the east and watch the Sun return to his people. When he comes to noon, go to the south and sit there, and when he has travelled low again, go to the west where you sat first and watch until he is gone. Then start for your home."

Page 115 **CHIEF JOSEPH—NEZ PERCÉ**

The name of Chief Joseph is better known than that of any other Northwestern Indian. To him popular opinion has given the credit of conducting a remarkable strategic movement from Idaho to northern Montana in the fight of the Nez Percés in 1877. . . . Their unfortunate effort to retain what was rightly their own makes an unparalleled story in the annals of the Indians' resistance to the greed of the whites. That they made this final effort is not surprising. Indeed, it is remarkable that so few tribes rose in a last struggle against such dishonest and relentless subjection.

Joseph was, in the minds of his people, more a peace chief than a war leader. . . . Joseph and somewhat more than a hundred of his people were sent to Nespilim, on the Colville reservation in eastern Washington. Joseph continued through the remainder of his life the hopeless plea for the Wallowa Valley, one of his last acts being a journey to Washington in one more effort. Perhaps it was discouragement, more likely it was intuition, but at any rate he seemed to know that his life was drawing to a close, for while returning to his home he told those with whom he talked that he would make no more journeys; he would soon be gone. And so it was. In the following year, on September 21, 1904, his life's fight closed.

Page 117 **NEW CHEST—PIEGAN**

The men of the Piegan tribe were organized into a series of warrior societies in which membership was based on age. The function of the societies was primarily to preserve order in the camp, during the march, on the hunt; to punish offenders against the public welfare; to protect the camp by guarding against possible surprise by an enemy; to be informed at all times as to the movements of the buffalo herds; and secondarily by inter-society rivalry to cultivate the military spirit, and by their feasts and dances to minister to the desire of members for social recreation.

Page 119 **A HOPI MAN**

In this physiognomy we read the dominant traits of Hopi character. The eyes speak of wariness, if not of downright distrust. The mouth shows great possibilities of unyielding stubbornness. Yet somewhere in this face lurks an expression of masked warmheartedness and humanity.

Page 121 **CLAYOQUOT GIRL**

Courting was done secretly. It was rather difficult to meet alone a girl of high birth, but to exchange whispered words and tokens in the night through the cracks in the wall was a simple matter; and if the suitor possessed the courage he could occasionally creep through the door into his sweetheart's presence. Parents were inclined to wink at the peccadilloes of their daughters. . . provided only the manner of the doing were not too overt. The girl who was trained to be so circumspect in the street that she would not lift an eye from the ground, who never left the village except in the company of her mother or a slave woman, that same damsel might in the dead of night receive more than one secret lover in her bedroom. But that was nothing to discredit so long as she maintained her circumspectness in public.

Page 123 **A CREE WOMAN**

The Cree, an important and well-known branch of the great Algonquian family are geographically and linguistically closely related to the Ojibway, or Chippewa. On the basis of habitat they are generally designated as Plains Cree and Woods, or Swamp, Cree. Bands of the former division roamed the prairies of Manitoba, Saskatchewan and eastern Alberta, where they are now sedentary on numerous small reserves. Their movement into the open country in pursuit of buffalo was westward up the Saskatchewan, which flows into Lake Winnipeg.

Page 125 **BEAR BULL—BLACKFOOT**

The plate illustrates an ancient Blackfoot method of arranging the hair.

Page 127 **HORSE CAPTURE,** ***WAATYANATH,*—ATSINA**

Born near Milk River in 1858. When about fifteen years of age he went with a war-party against the Piegan, but achieved no honor. From their camp at Beaver creek the Atsina sent out a war-party which came upon two Sioux. Remaining hidden in a coulee, the warriors sent an old man out as decoy. When the Sioux charged him, the rest of the Atsina rushed and killed them both. During the fight Horse Capture ran up to one of the enemy, who was wounded, in order to count coup, when one of his companions dashed in ahead of him and was killed by the wounded Sioux. Horse Capture then counted first coup on the enemy and killed him.

Page 129 **BEAR'S TEETH—ARIKARA**

A member of the Night order of the medicine fraternity. The distinctive rite of the Arikara was that of the medicine fraternity, *Shunúwanúh*, Magic Performance. This lasted from mid-summer into the fall, with singing and dancing and performance of legerdemain in the lodge every afternnoon and night.

Page 131 **A HOPI MOTHER**

When a Hopi child is about to be born, the father's paternal grandmother, or, if she be dead or incapable of acting, his paternal aunt, brings a bowl of water and an ear of corn. The prospective mother lies on a bed of sand, and when the child is delivered the attendant receives it, cuts the umbilical cord, washes the infant in the bowl of water, and wraps it in clothes heated to such a temperature as they think sufficient to kill any vermin therein. She then lays the child on a tray basket, places beside it the ear of corn, which is called its "Mother", and carries out the placenta and fetal envelopes, casts them over the cliff upon the piles of refuse, and tosses after them a pinch of meal. For twenty days the room is kept darkened, the door being screened with a shawl or a blanket: for the rays of the sun must not shine on the mother during this period.

Page 133 **A SON OF THE DESERT—NAVAHO**

In the early morning this boy, as if springing from the earth itself, came to the author's desert camp. Indeed, he seemed a part of the very desert. His eyes bespeak all the curiosity, all the wonder of his primitive mind striving to grasp the meaning of the strange things about him.

Page 135 **THE POTTER MIXING CLAY**

This woman, so aged that her shrivelled skin hangs in folds, still finds pleasure in creating artistic and utilitarian pieces of pottery.

Pottery and basketry are the work of women. Pottery vessels are built up by the process of coiling a rope of plastic clay upon itself and are fired in a burning mound of sheep-dung. . . . All cooking-vessels, food dishes, and water jars are pottery. . . .

The potter's clay is dug out from under the rocks about the foothills of the mesa. When thoroughly dry it is ground on the mealing stones, and after it has soaked in water a quantity of pulverized sandstone or potsherds is mixed with it. Ancient, decorated sherds are preferred for this purpose, fragments of cooking-pots not being used.

Page 137 **THE STORM—APACHE**

A scene in the high mountains of Apache-land just before the breaking of a rainstorm.

Page 139 **A BLACKFOOT TRAVOIS**

The travois is still used for transporting bundles of ceremonial objects. Before, and sometimes even long after, the acquisition of horses, travoix were drawn by dogs. The travois consisted of two lodge-poles with a rawhide seat lashed between them. When dogs were used the travois was of course small, and lodge-poles could not be employed.

Page 141 AN IDLE HOUR—PIEGAN

In disposition the Piegan are particularly tractable and like-able. One can scarcely find a tribe so satisfactory to work among. In the old days of primitive customs and laws, they were fond of formality, especially in their social relations, and these exactions were, of course, largely a part of their religion. A noteworthy phase of such form in their daily and hourly life was the excessive use of the pipe. On lighting it they touched it to the earth and held it to the sky, in silent prayer to the spirits—the earth-people and the sky-people. Each serious act of their waking day was preceded by similar formal smoking. They did not confine their religious observances to a fixed time or place, but rather were constantly in act or thought supplicating the Infinite.

Page 143 KUTENAI DUCK HUNTER

In the gray dawn of a foggy morning the hunter crouches in his canoe among the rushes, waiting for the water-fowl to come within range.

Page 145 PIEGAN ENCAMPMENT

This picture not only presents a characteristic view of an Indian camp on an uneventful day, but also emphasizes the grand picturesqueness of the environment of the Piegan, living as they do almost under the shadow of the towering Rocky mountains.

Page 147 WICHITA GRASS-HOUSE

The Wichita erected substantial, conical, grass-thatched dwellings which served also as ceremonial lodges. An elaborate ritual accompanied their erection. For summer use rectangular arbors were built, the roof thatched in a manner similar to that of the grass-house, but the sides were left open. Maidens slept in a thatched hut built on a platform reached by a ladder which was removed at night when the girls retired.

The relatively permanent character of the typical dwelling of the Wichita indicates the sedentary life of the tribe. They were farmers in the main but hunted the buffalo and other game.

Page 149 GATHERING TULES—LAKE POMO

The round-stem tule, *Scirpus lacustris*, was used principally for thatching houses, for making mats by stringing them laterally on parallel cords and, securely as lashed together in long bundles, in the construction of serviceable and quickly made canoes.

Page 151 A MONO HOME

The Mono inhabit east-central California from Owens lake to the head of the southerly affluents of Walker river. The snow-capped Sierra Nevada rises abruptly on the western border of this inland basin.

The Mono house was approximately hemispherical, twelve to fourteen feet in diameter with an excavated floor, and without supporting posts. Willow poles slightly bent to meet at the top formed the frame work, and the thatch was grass or rushes.

The wickiup shown in the plate is a typical winter shelter, and the utensils are burden-baskets and sieves, or winnowing-trays.

Page 153 ON THE SHORES AT NOOTKA

Two women wearing the primitive bark blanket and nose-ornament, and with clam-baskets on their backs, rest on the beach while waiting for the tide to fall and uncover the clam-beds.

Page 155 A HAIDA CHIEF'S TOMB AT YAN

The remains of the chief rest in a niche cut into the top of the transverse beam. This tomb is of unusual form, and must have been erected at enormous cost to the dead man's family.

Page 157 HOMEWARD

Page 159 A NOOTKA MAN

It is commonly believed that the facial hair of many North Coast natives is proof of intermingled Caucasian blood; but that such is not the case is conclusively proved by the statement of Captain Cook, who in 1778 observed that "some of them, and particularly the old men, have not only considerable beards all over the chin, but whiskers, or mustachios."

Page 161 WOMAN AND CHILD—NUNIVAK

Children and adults alike of the Nunivak group are healthy, as a rule and exceptionally happy because they have been little affected by contact with civilization.

Sealing is of prime importance to the people of Nunivak island, the seal being sought in spring and in fall during their northward and southward migrations respectively.

Page 163 CHEYENNE TYPE

The original of this portrait is Wakó'yami (His Horse Bobtailed), of the Northern Cheyenne.

Page 165 WISHHAM GIRL

The subject is clothed in a heavily beaded deerskin dress of the plains type. The throat is encircled by strands of shell beads of native manufacture, heirlooms which were obtained by the original Wishham possessor from the Pacific slope. Pendent on the breast are strands of larger beads of the same kind, as well as of various kinds brought into the country by the traders of the Hudson's Bay Cmpany. An indispensable ornament of the well-born person was the dentalium shell thrust through a perforation in the nasal septum; occasionally, as in this case, two such shells were connected by means of a bit of wool pushed into the hollow bases. Tied to the hair at each side of face is another dentalium-shell ornament, which is in reality an ear-pendant transferred from the lobe of the ear (where its weight would be inconvenient) to the hair. The head-dress consists of shells, shell beads, commercial beads, and Chinese coins. The coins made their appearance in the Columbia River region at a comparatively early date. This form of head-dress was worn on special occasions by girls between the age of puberty and their marriage.

Page 167 A ZUÑI GOVERNOR

The principal civil officers, governor and lieutenant-governor, are appointed annually by a group of the head-priests. Formerly the term was four years. These civil officers, a Spanish heritage, deal mainly with strictly secular affairs, a limited field in a community where one ceremony follows closely upon another. The real power resides in four hierarchical groups: the six head-priests associated with the six world-regions, the principals of the fraternity of masked personators of gods, the war-chiefs, and the shamanistic societies.

Page 169 RED CLOUD—OGALALA

Well-known chief and celebrated warrior. Born 1822. At the age of fifteen he accompanied a war-party which killed eighty Pawnee. He took two scalps and shot one man. At seventeen he led a party that killed eight of the same tribe. During his career he killed two Shoshoni and ten Apsaroke. Once going against the Apsaroke, he led the party and approached the camp on foot. About daylight a man came driving his herd to the range. Red Cloud charged him, killed him with arrows, stabbed him with the Apsaroke's own knife, and scalped him; he then took his clothes and started back, driving the horses. Men from the camp pursued, and a severe fight followed between the two parties. . . . Red Cloud received his name in recognition of his bravery, from his father after the latter's death. Before that his name had been Two Arrows, *Wa-no pa*. His brother-in-law, Nachili, gave him medicine tied up in a little deerskin bag. Always before going to war Red Cloud rubbed this over his body. All the tribe regarded his medicine as very potent. He first gained notice as a leader by his success at Fort Phil. Kearny in 1866 when he killed Captain Fetterman and eighty soldiers. In the following year he led a large party, two or three thousand, it is said, in an attack on a wood-train at the same post, but was repulsed with great loss. Previously only chief of the Bad Face band of Ogalala, he became head-chief of the tribe after the abandonment of Fort Phil. Kearny. Red Cloud was prevented from joining in the Custer fight by the action of General Mackenzie in disarmimng him and his camp.

Page 171 MÓSA—MOHAVE

It would be difficult to conceive of a more thorough aboriginal than this Mohave girl. Her eyes are those of the fawn of the forest, questioning the strange things of civilization upon which it gazes for the first time. She is such a type as Father Garcés may have viewed on his journey through the Mohave country in 1776.

Page 173 GERONIMO—APACHE

This portrait of the historical old Apache was made in March 1905. According to Geronimo's calculation he was at that time seventy-six years of age, thus making the year of his birth 1829. The picture was taken at Carlisle, Pennsylvania, the day before the inauguration of President Roosevelt, Geronimo being one of the warriors who took part in the inaugural parade at Washington. He appreciated the honor of being one of those chosen for this occasion, and the catching of his features while the old warrior was in a retrospective mood was most fortunate.

Page 175 THE THREE CHIEFS—PIEGAN

Three proud old leaders of their people—Four Horns, Small Leggings and Mountain Chief. A picture of the primal upland prairies of Montana with their waving grass and limpid streams. A glimpse of the life and conditions which are on the verge of extinction.

THE RUSH GATHERER – KUTENAI

THE BLANKET WEAVER - NAVAHO

CAÑON DE CHELLY - NAVAHO

FOR A WINTER CAMPAIGN - APSAROKE

KWAKIUTL HOUSE-FRAME

14

KÓTSUIS AND HÓHHUQ - NAKOAKTOK

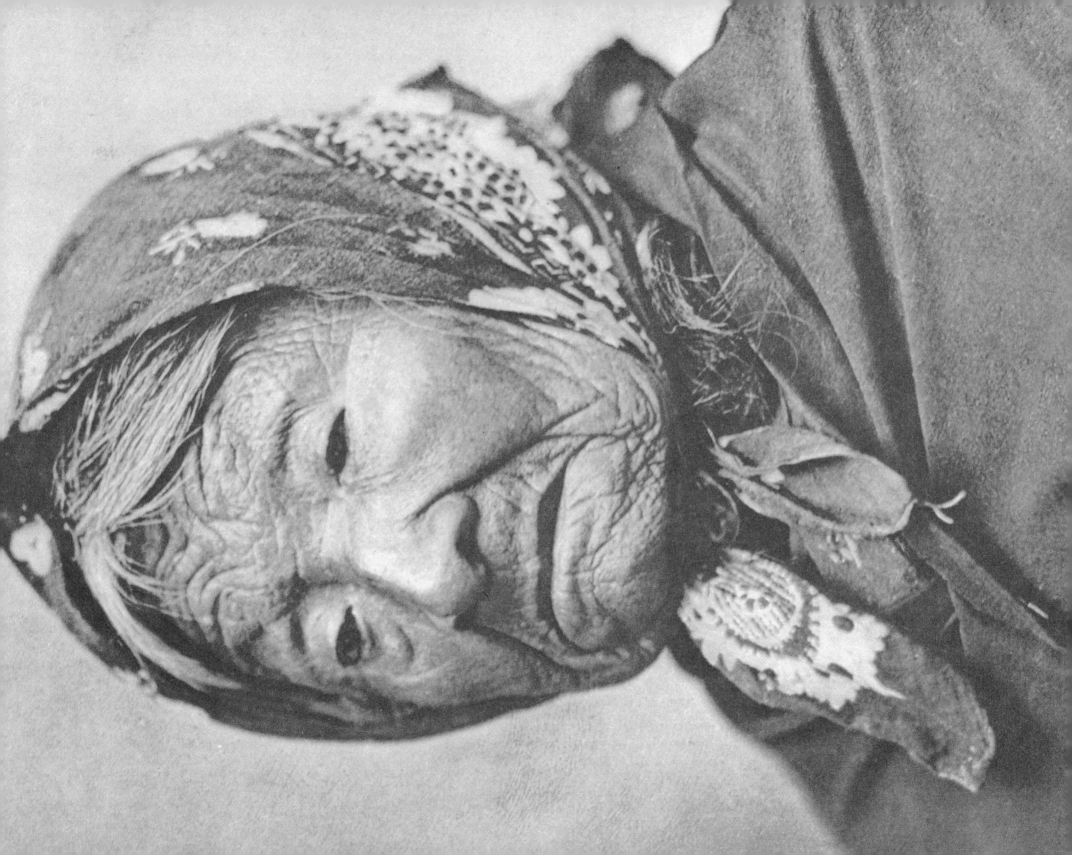

APIÓ-MITA ("WHITE DOG") — BLOOD

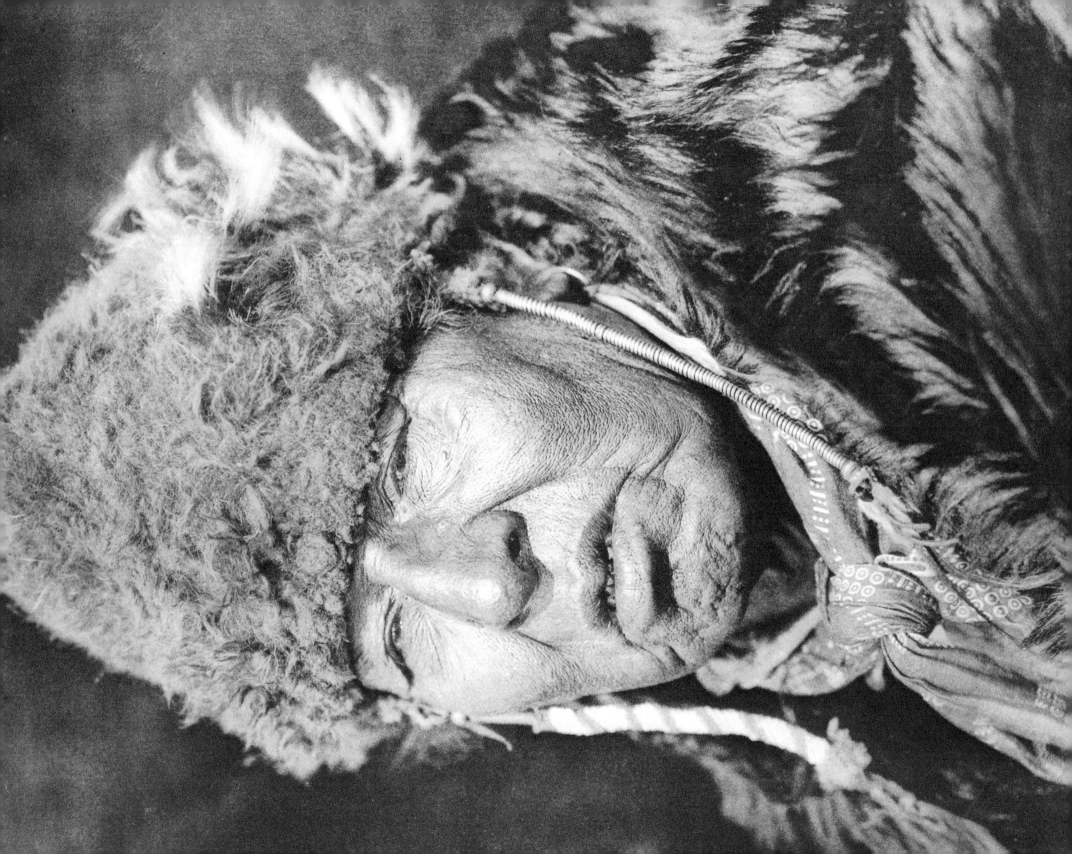

QAHÁTĬKA GIRL

24

OGALALA WOMAN

32

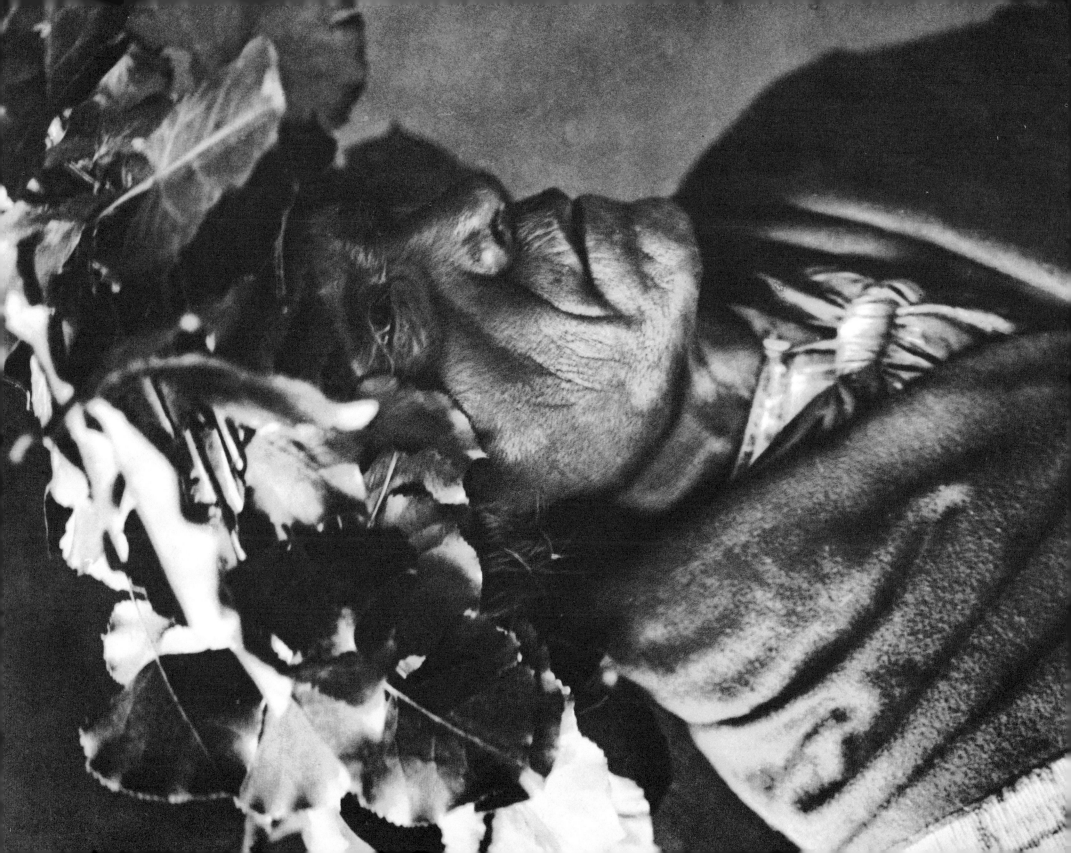

34

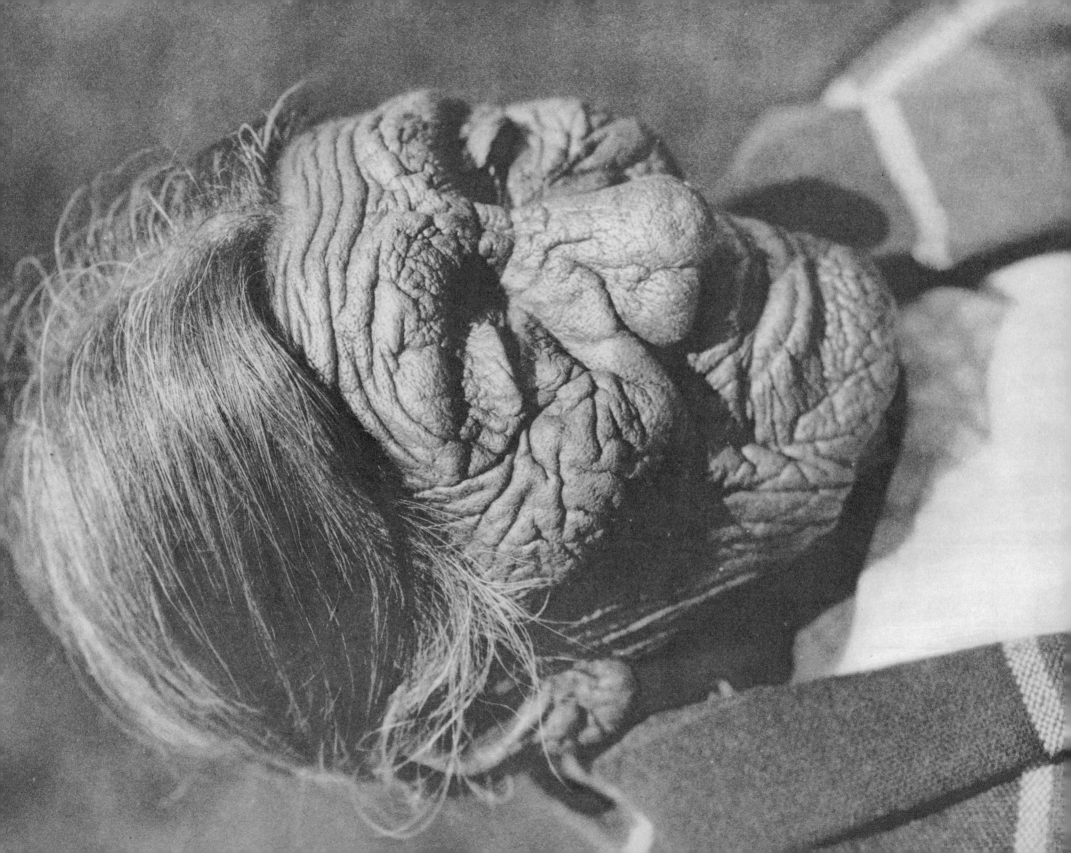

CHEYENNE GIRL

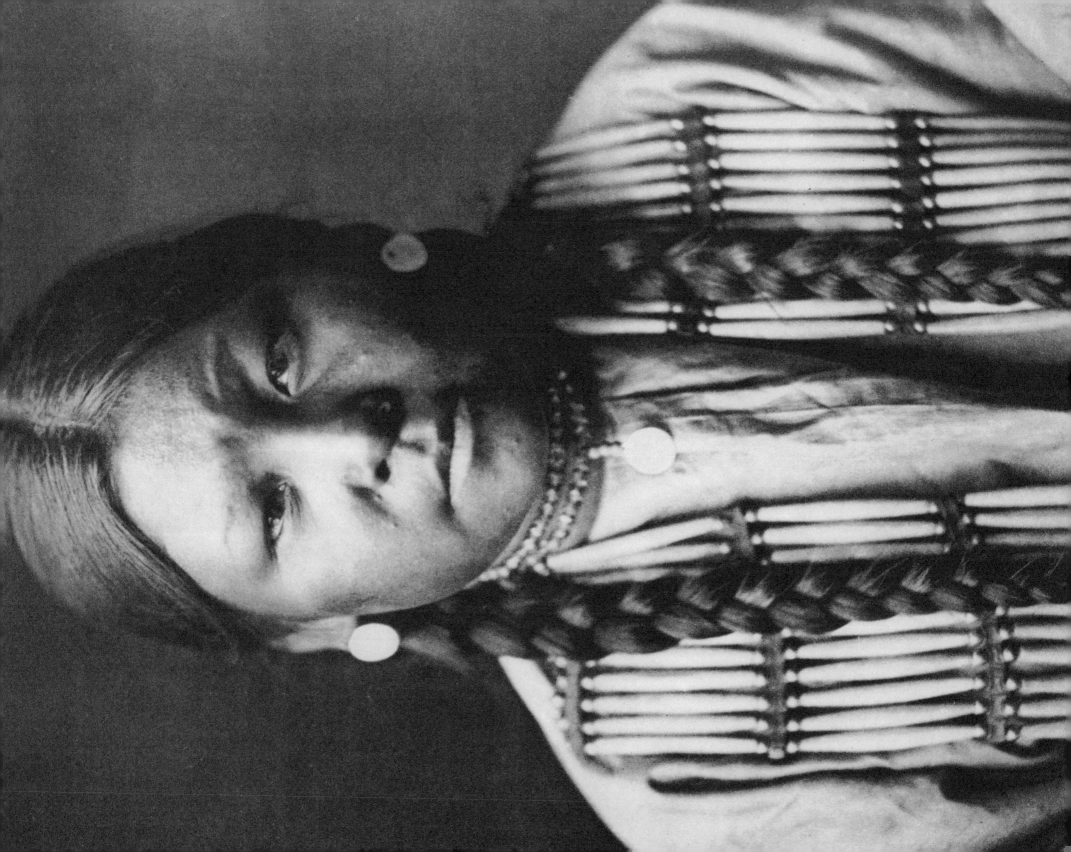

THE WHALER - MAKAH

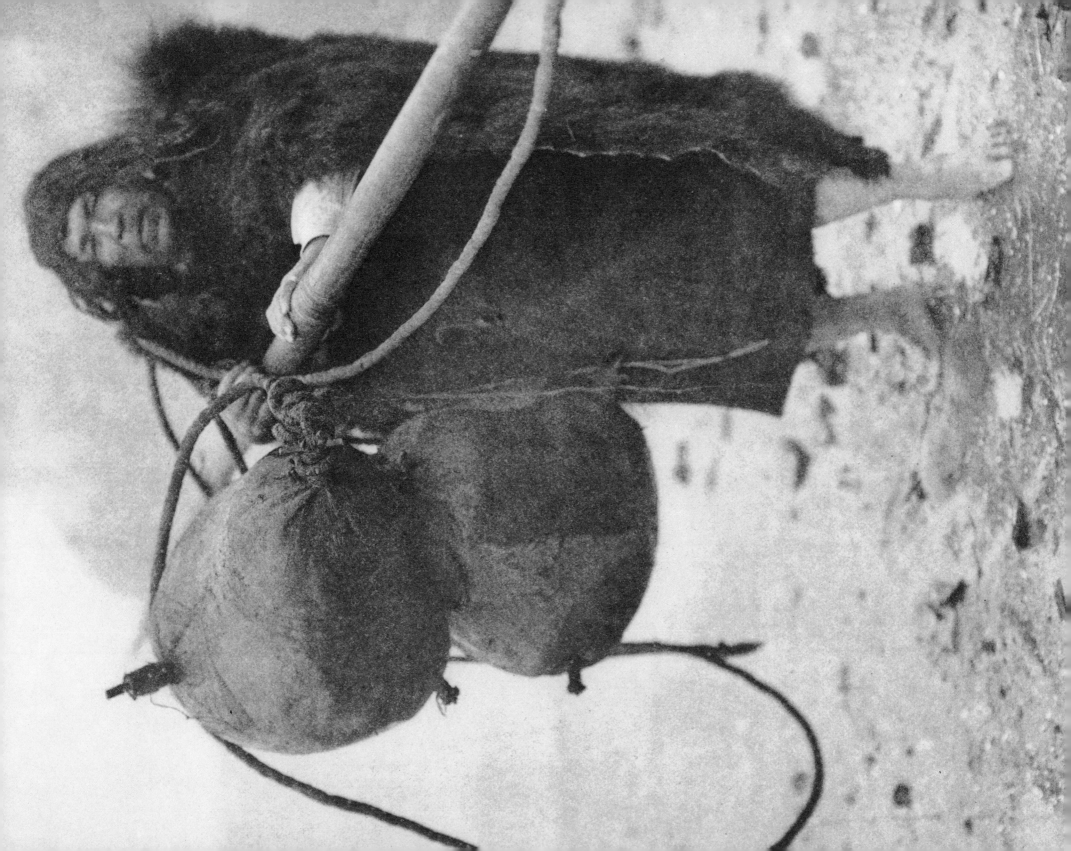

NOOTKA METHOD OF SPEARING

A NAKOAKTOK CHIEF'S DAUGHTER

HESQUIAT ROOT DIGGER

48

A HEAVY LOAD - SIOUX

WAITING IN THE FOREST - CHEYENNE

A MOUNTAIN FASTNESS - APSAROKE

A FEAST DAY AT ACOMA

WASHING WHEAT — SAN JUAN

WALPI

ANTELOPES AND SNAKES AT ORAIBI

ZUÑI GIRLS AT THE RIVER

A HOPI GIRL

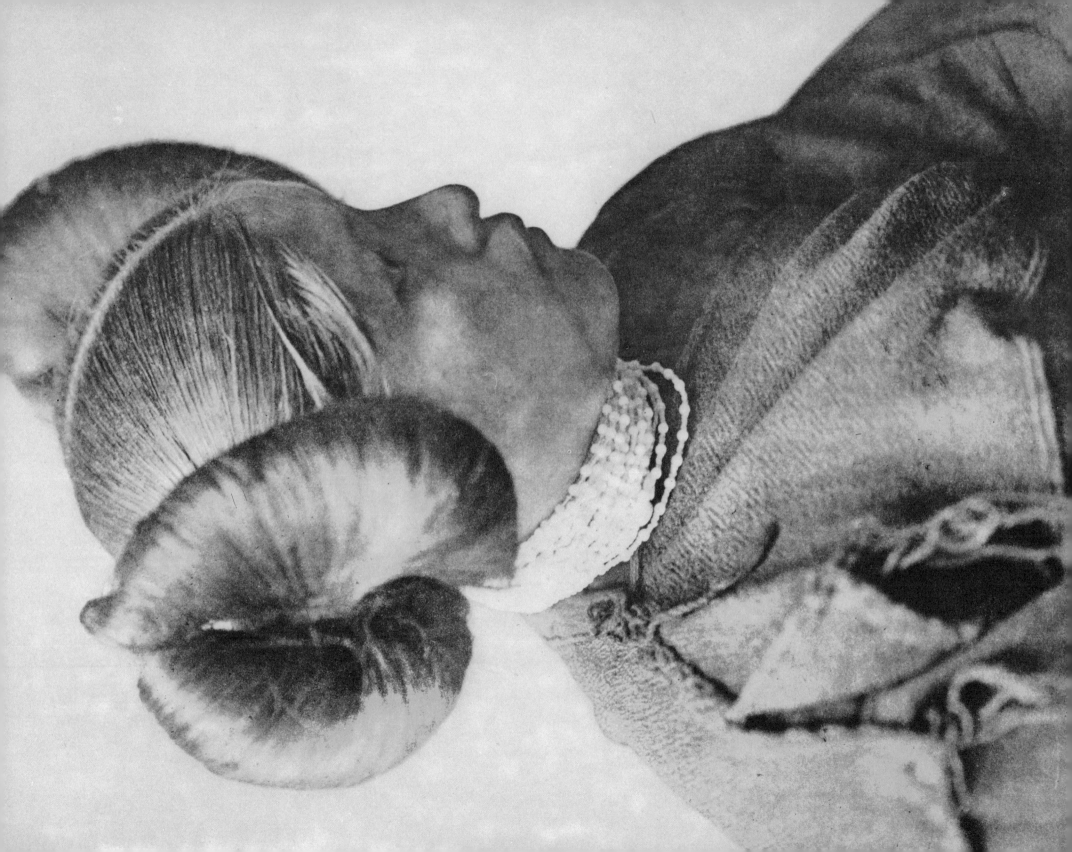

ANDRÉS CAÑON

AN APACHE BABE

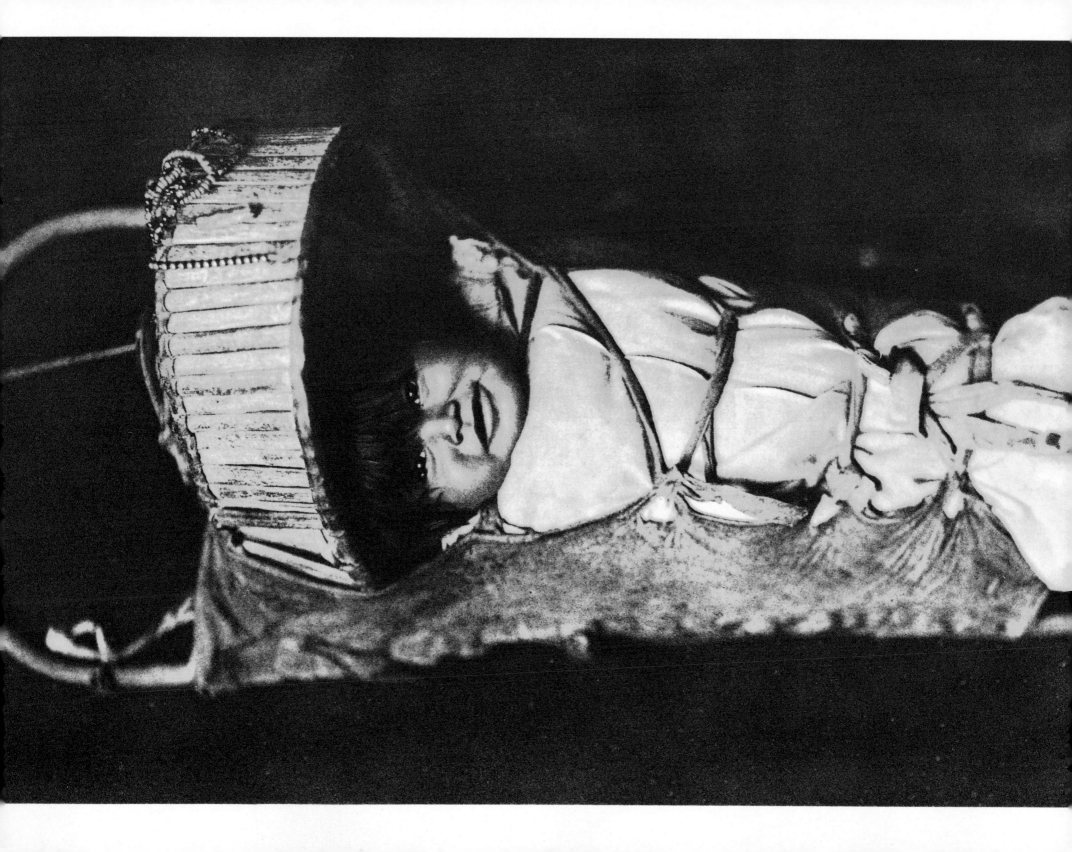

GETTING WATER - APACHE

AS IT WAS IN THE OLD DAYS

HUPA TROUT-TRAP

CANOE OF TULES — POMO

ON SPOKANE RIVER

PIMA KI

ASSINIBOIN MOTHER AND CHILD

ATSINA WARRIORS

ON THE LITTLE BIGHORN - APSAROKE

FISHING CAMP — LAKE POMO

THE OFFERING – SAN ILDEFONSO

NEZ PERCÉ BABE

CHIEF JOSEPH - NEZ PERCÉ

A HOPI MAN

A CREE WOMAN

BEAR BULL—BLACKFOOT

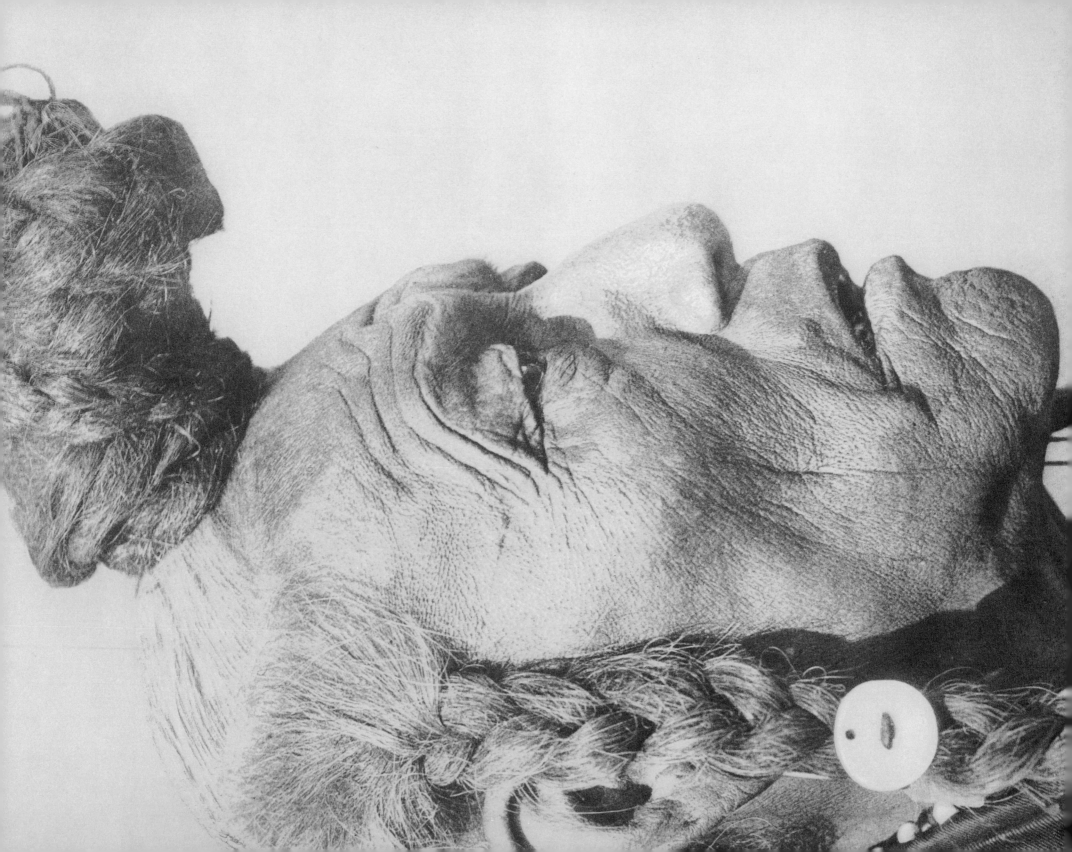

HORSE CAPTURE - ATSINA

BEAR'S TEETH – ARIKARA

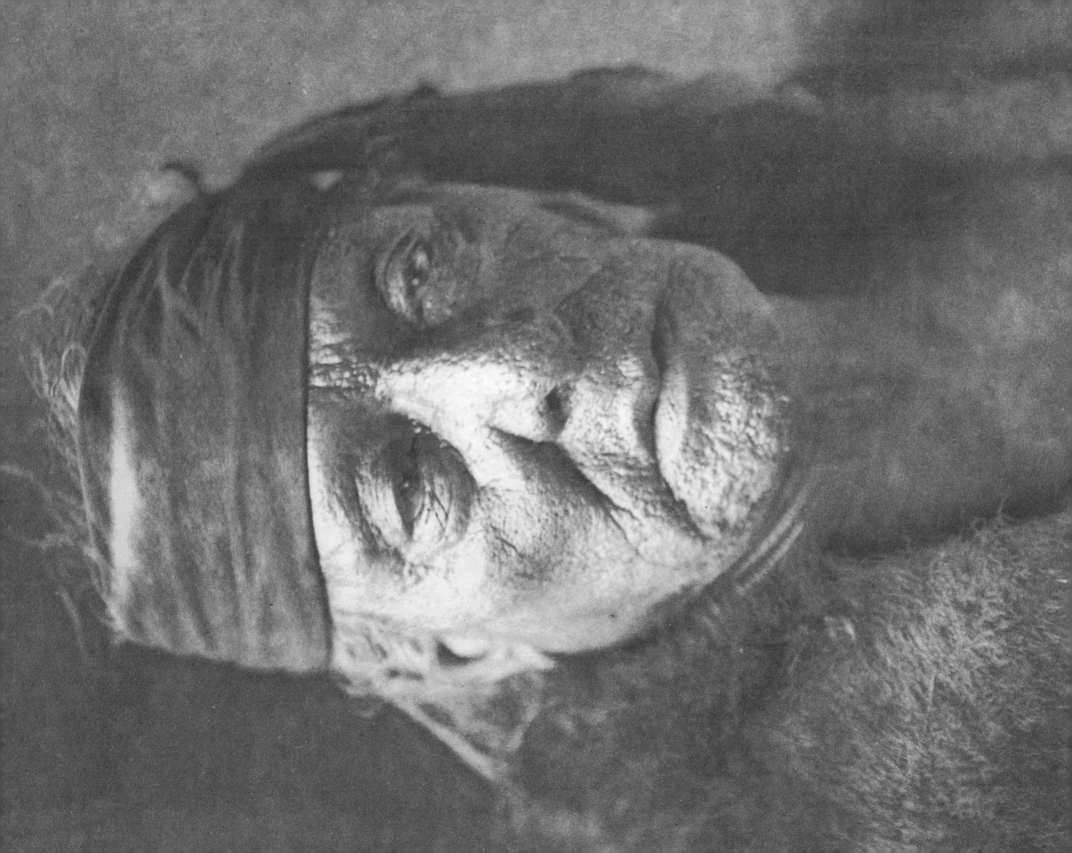

A HOPI MOTHER

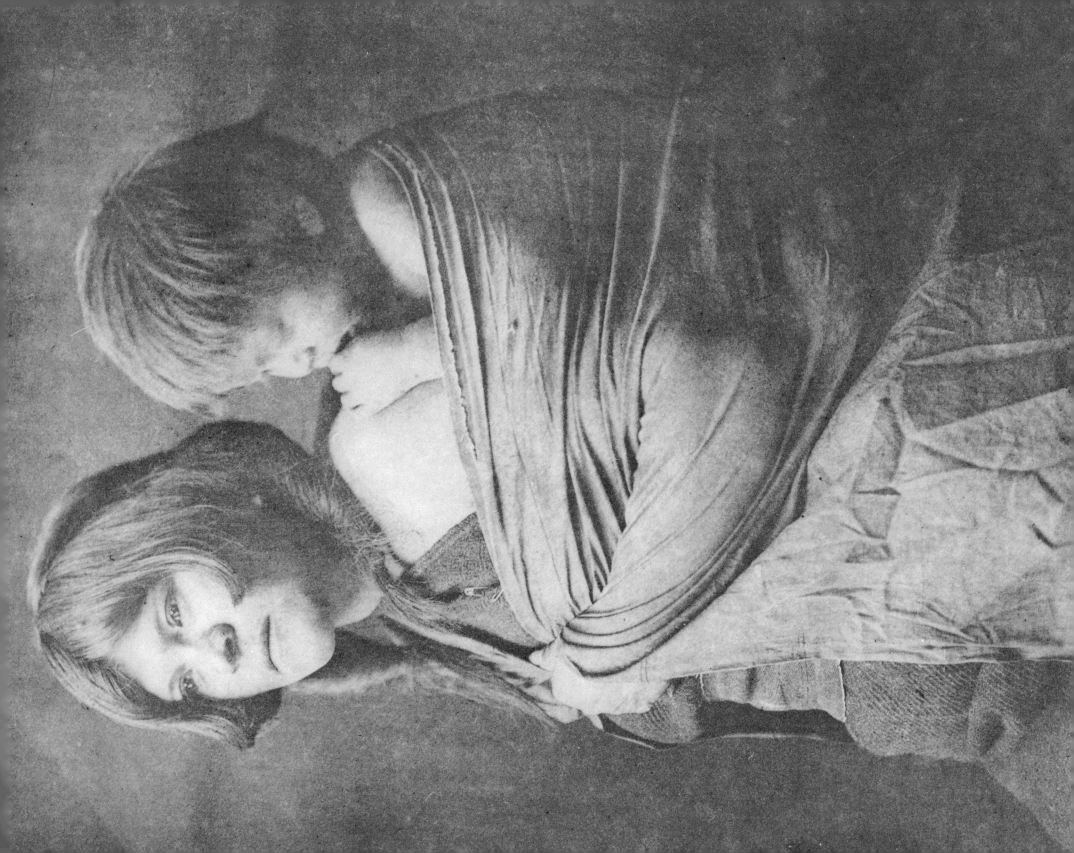

A SON OF THE DESERT - NAVAHO

THE STORM - APACHE

A BLACKFOOT TRAVOIS

140

GATHERING TULES — LAKE POMO

A MONO HOME

ON THE SHORES AT NOOTKA

A HAIDA CHIEF'S TOMB AT YAN

A NOOTKA MAN

WOMAN AND CHILD — NUNIVAK

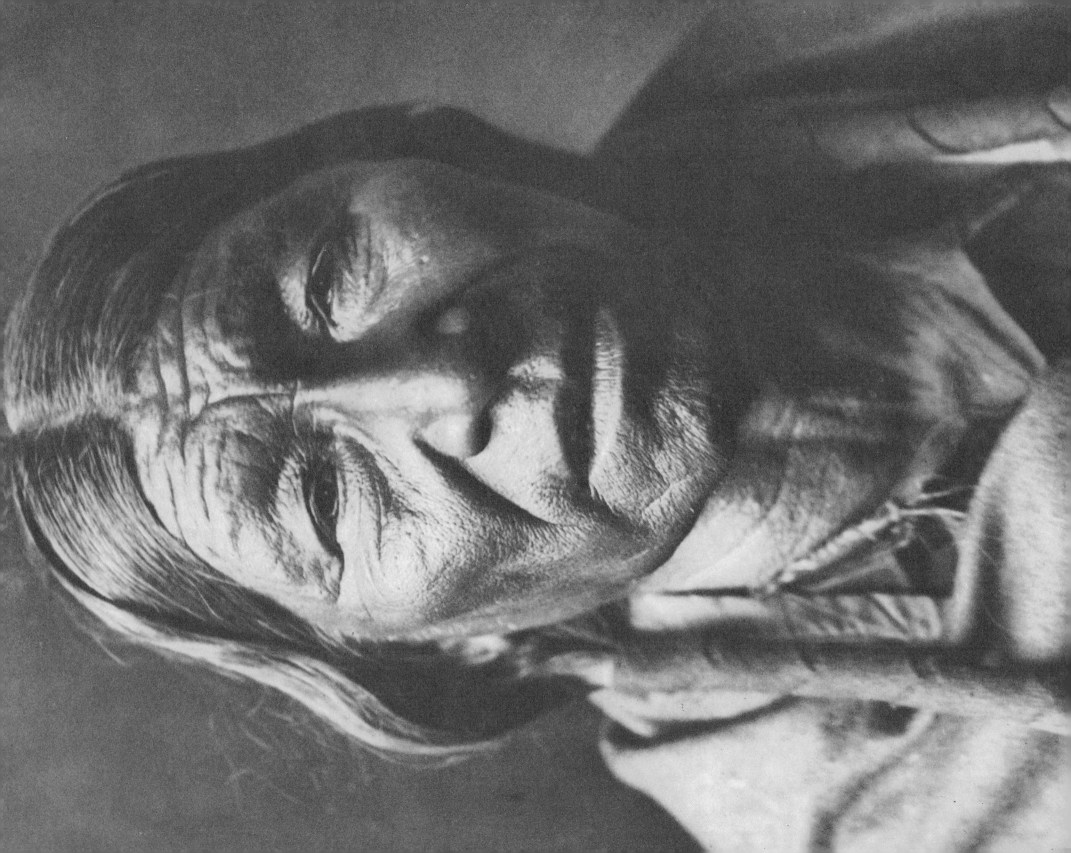

WISHHAM GIRL

A ZUÑI GOVERNOR

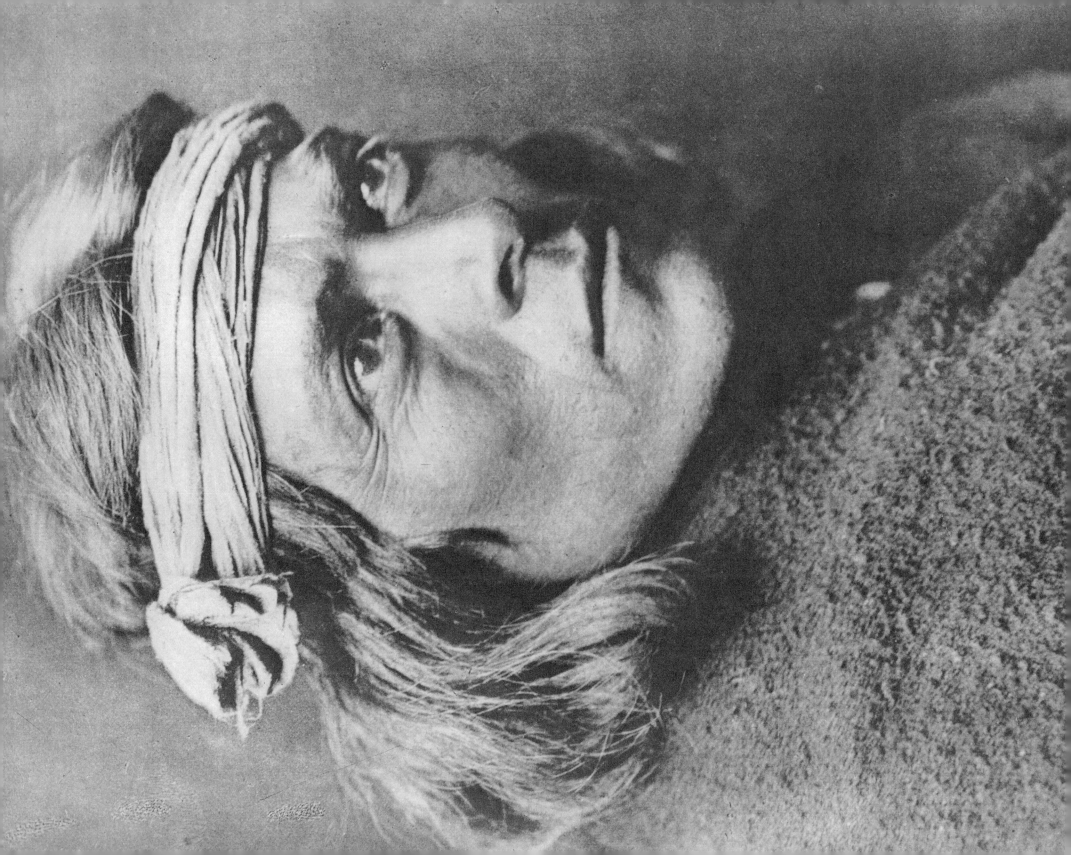

RED CLOUD – OGALALA

MÓSA - MOHAVE

GERONIMO - APACHE

THE THREE CHIEFS - PIEGAN